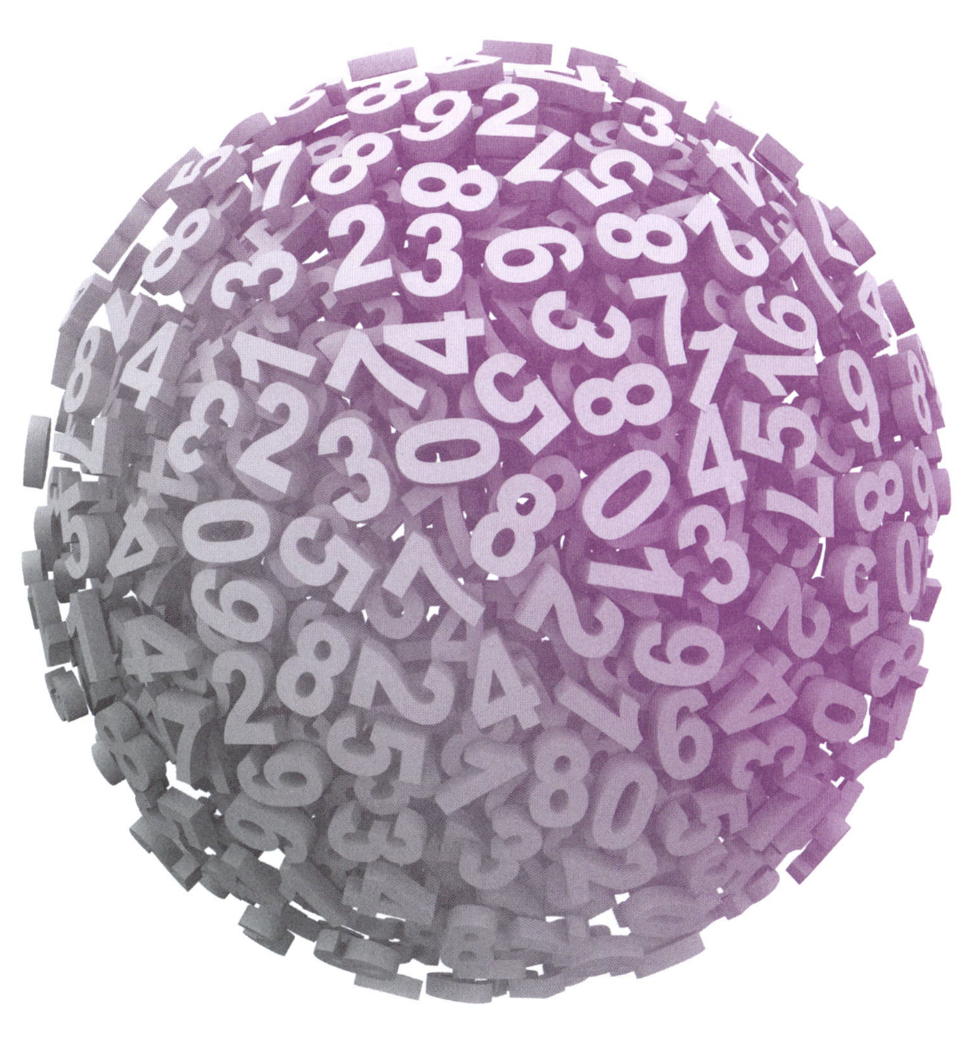

NUMBER

Walker Maths Essentials: Number 4+
1st Edition
Charlotte Walker
Victoria Walker

Designer: Cheryl Smith, Macarn Design
Production controller: Magda Koralewska

Any URLs contained in this publication were checked for currency during the production process. Note, however, that the publisher cannot vouch for the ongoing currency of URLs.

Acknowledgements
Cover photo courtesy of Shutterstock.
We wish to thank the Boards of Trustees of Darfield and Riccarton High Schools for allowing us to use materials and ideas developed while teaching. Our thanks also go to all past and present colleagues, especially Kath Wilson, who have generously shared their experience and ideas.

For product information and technology assistance,
in Australia call **1300 790 853**;
in New Zealand call **0800 449 725**

For permission to use material from this text or product, please email
aust.permissions@cengage.com

National Library of New Zealand Cataloguing-in-Publication Data
A catalogue record for this book is available from the National Library of New Zealand.

978 0 170447379

Cengage Learning Australia
Level 7, 80 Dorcas Street
South Melbourne, Victoria Australia 3205

For learning solutions, visit **cengage.co.nz**

Printed in China by 1010 Printing International Limited.
5 6 7 24

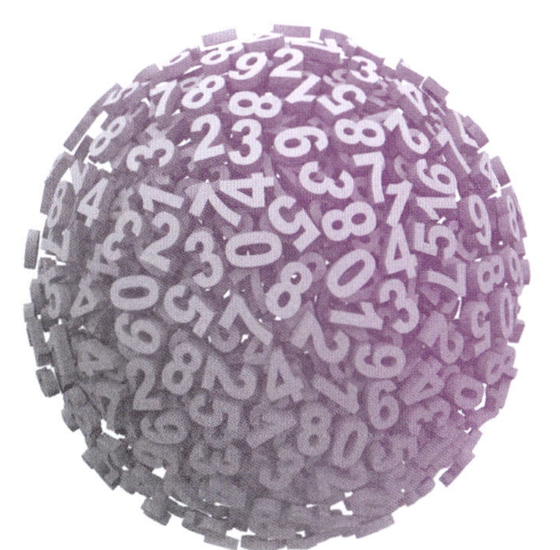

CONTENTS

Glossary

Make your own glossary of key terms:

Term	Definition	Picture/Example
BEDMAS		
Integers		
Multiple		
Lowest common multiple (LCM)		
Factor		
Highest common factor (HCF)		
Prime number		
Square root		
Consecutive		

ISBN: 9780170447379

Numerator		
Denominator		
Mixed fraction		
Improper fraction		
Reciprocal		
Equivalent fraction		
Place value		
Decimal place		
Exponent		

ISBN: 9780170447379

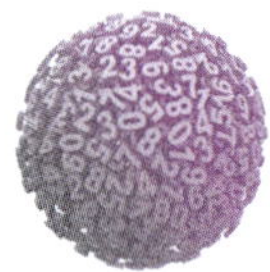

The language of mathematics

Words to operations

Write down the most appropriate operation (**+**, **−**, **x** or **÷**) for each of the following terms.

	Terms	Operations
1	What is three **more than** ten?	+
2	Find a half **of** twelve.	
3	Find the result when six is **reduced** by two.	
4	What is seven **times** four?	
5	If ten is **decreased by** six, what is the result?	
6	Find fourteen **divided by** two.	
7	Calculate eight **less than** eleven.	
8	Find the **sum of** five and seven.	
9	Calculate three **and** one.	
10	What is twelve **shared between** six?	
11	Twenty-two is **added** to four.	
12	What is twenty **increased by** eight?	
13	Find a number that is **smaller than** thirteen.	
14	What is eighteen **plus** four?	
15	Calculate the **difference between** eight and five.	
16	What is the **product** of three and nine?	
17	What is fifteen **take away** eight?	
18	Ten **subtracted** from twenty-five.	
19	Find six **multiplied by** three.	
20	What is the **total of** fourteen and two?	

ISBN: 9780170447379

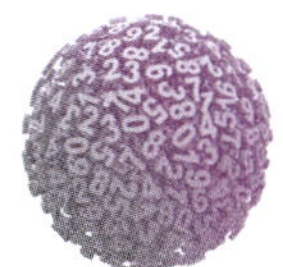

Integers

Adding and subtracting

- **–** means move **left**.
- **+** means move **right**.
- Remember that **– – = +**.

Do this on a number line.

Example: 2 – –4 – 7 = **2 + 4 – 7**
= –1

– – ⇒ +

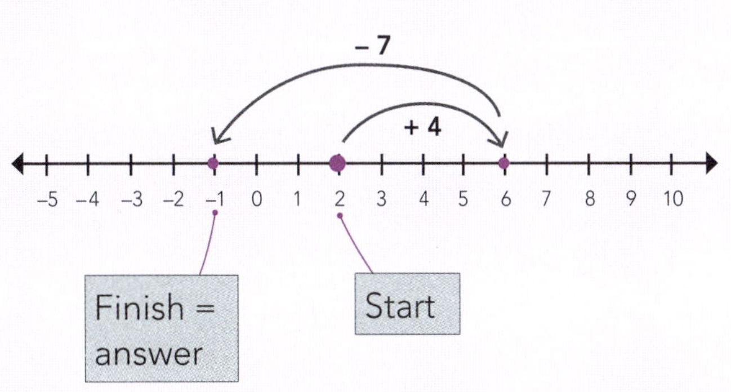

Add arrows and dots to these number lines in order to complete the calculations.

1 –3 + 8 =

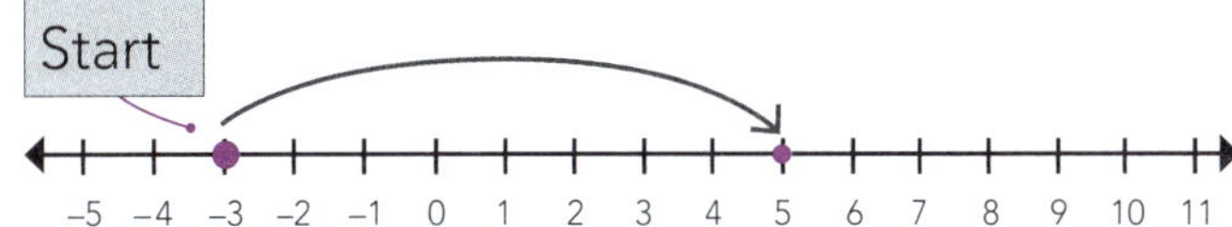

2 –2 – 4 =

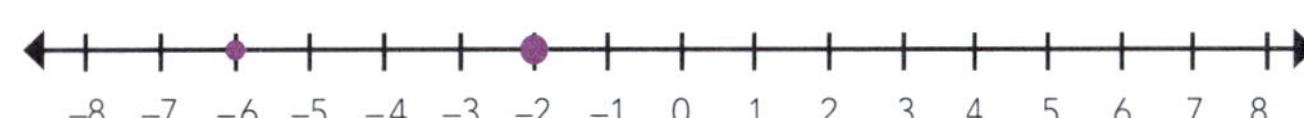

3 1 – –4 – 10 =

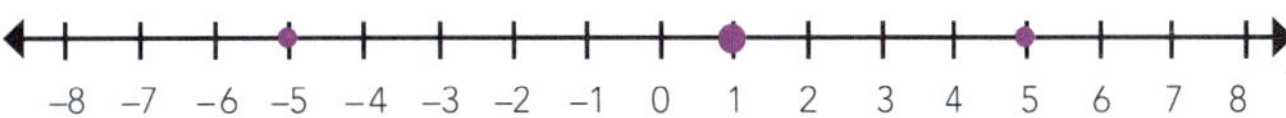

4 –2 + 9 – 4 =

5 –4 – –6 + 5 =

6 –7 + 3 – 2 – –3 =

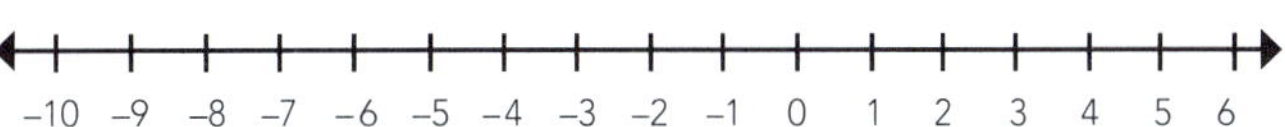

ISBN: 9780170447379

Complete the calculations.

7 −10 + 11 = ______________

8 2 − 7 = ______________

9 −2 + 7 − 8 = ______________

10 −5 − 1 + 8 = ______________

11 1 − −5 + 2 = ______________

12 6 + −1 + −5 = ______________

Write + or − signs in the boxes in order to create true statements.

13 □ 8 □ 3 = 5

14 □ 9 □ 2 = 7

15 □ 4 □ 6 = −2

16 □ 7 □ 10 □ 4 = 1

17 □ 6 □ 3 □ 9 = 0

18 You should be able to find several answers to this:

□ 5 □ 4 □ 3 □ 2 □ 1 = 1

□ 5 □ 4 □ 3 □ 2 □ 1 = 1

Place these values in ascending order.

19 14 ~~3~~ −7 0 −2 −5 9 −10

Smallest							Largest
					3		

20 −1 2 −9 −4 −2 6 8 −8

Smallest							Largest

21 12 21 −12 −21 −2 2 −1 1

Smallest							Largest

ISBN: 9780170447379

Integers on number lines

Here is how to work out the size of each gap between ticks on a number line.

Step 1: Calculate the **distance** between two **labelled** points.
Distance = 12 – –2 = **14**.

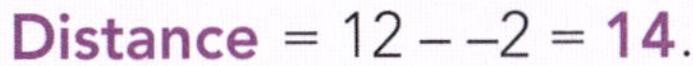
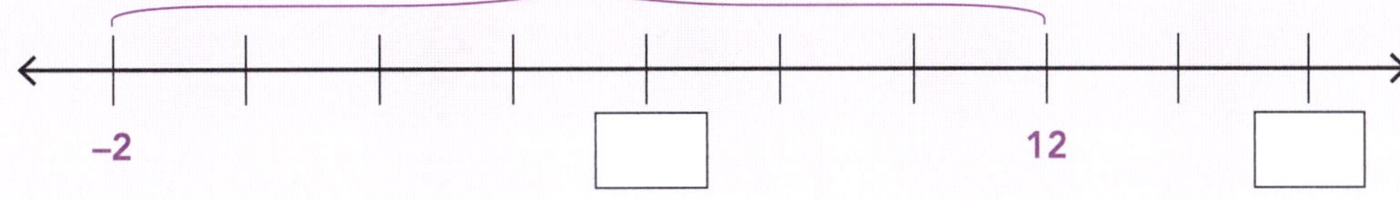

Step 2: Count the number of gaps between –2 and 12. **Number of gaps = 7**.

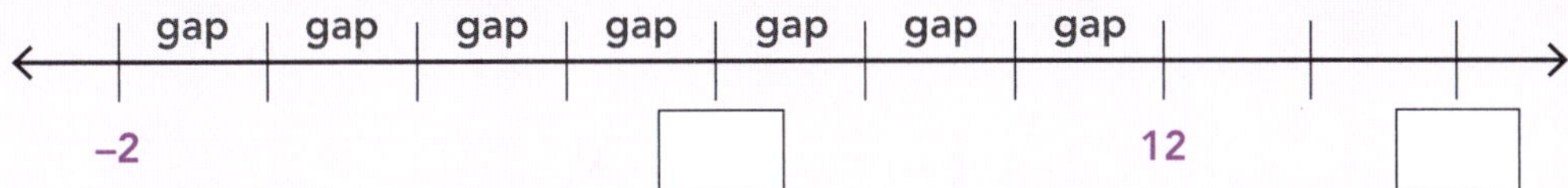

Step 3: Divide the distance by the number of gaps: $\frac{14}{7} = 2$.

Step 4: Add 2 after each gap along the number line.

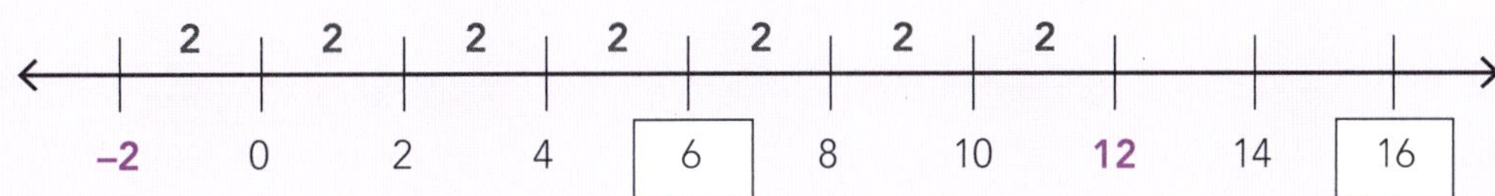

Calculate the size of each gap and write the missing integers on the number lines.

1

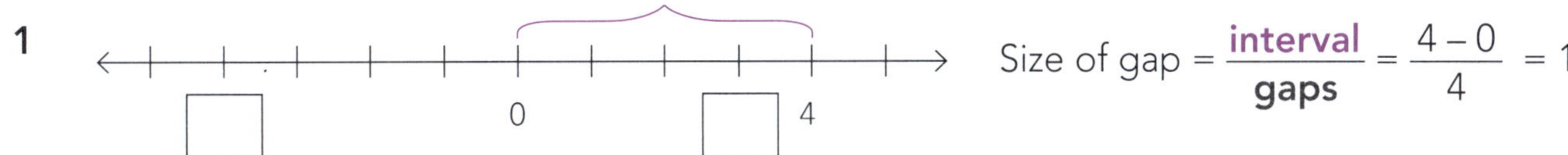

Size of gap = $\frac{\textbf{interval}}{\textbf{gaps}} = \frac{4-0}{4} = 1$

2

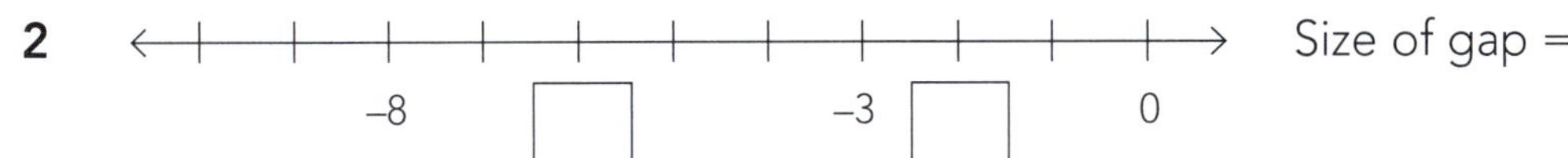

Size of gap =

3

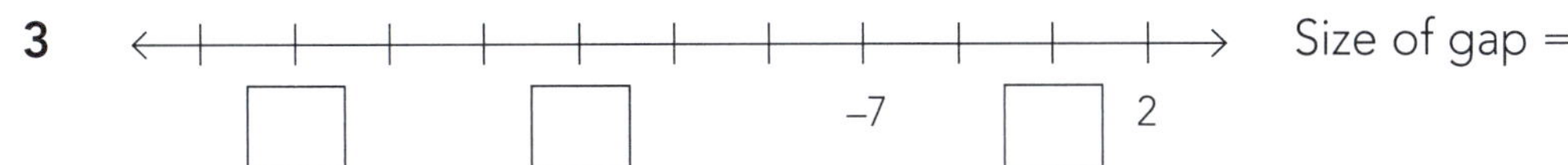

Size of gap =

4

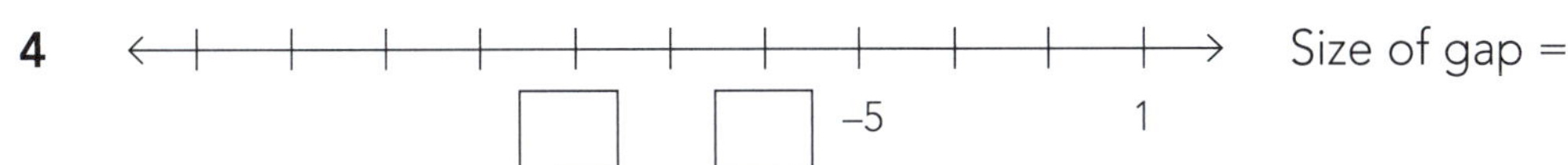

Size of gap =

5

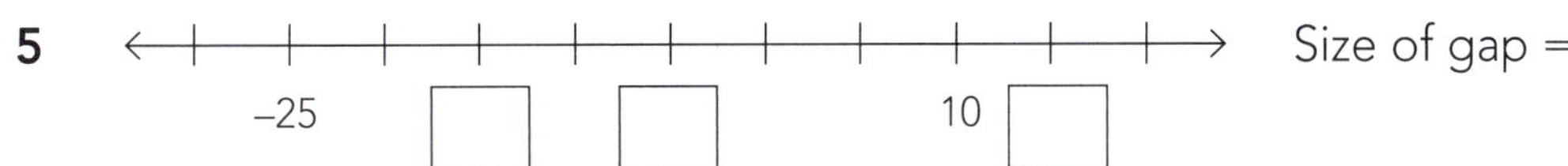

Size of gap =

6 Write the integer values for each point along the number line. Choose the most appropriate values from the list below. You will not need all the points on the list.

–9	–4	–18	–6	–11	1
–17	–3	–14	–1	–12	–13
–19	–7	–16	–15	–2	6

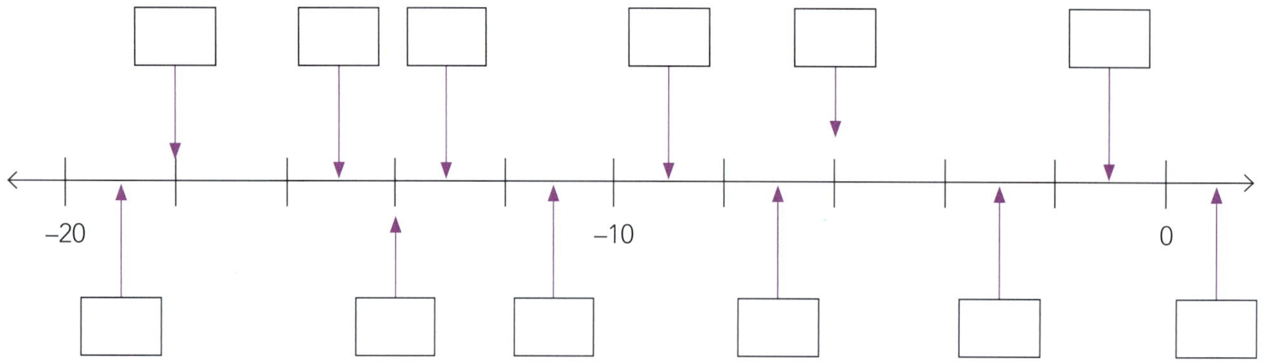

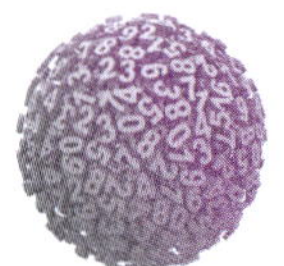

Challenge 1

1 Write integer values for each point along the number line. Choose the most appropriate values from the list below. You will not need all the points on the list.

–1	3	–15	–5	–25	–7
–21	–23	1	–29	–9	–24
–13	–17	–19	–33	–3	–31

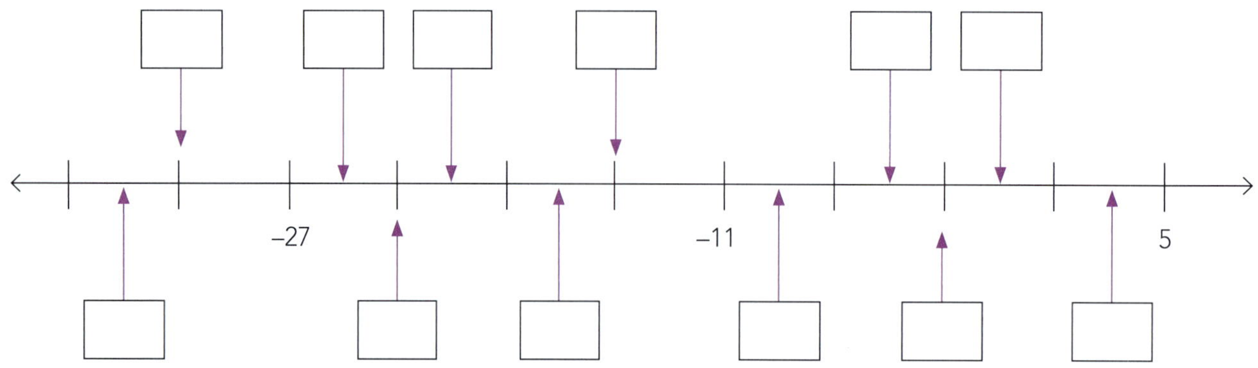

ISBN: 9780170447379

Multiplying and dividing

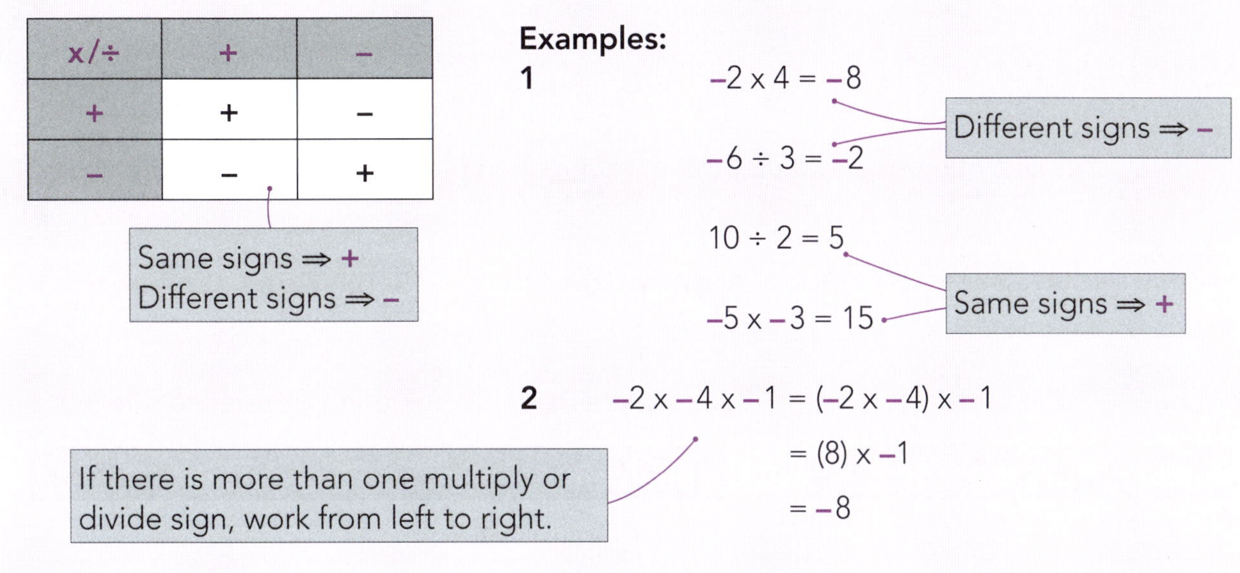

Highlight the correct answer for each of the following.

1	–3 x –4	12	7
		–7	–12
3	–3 x 3	9	0
		–6	–9
5	5 x 4 x –1	20	–10
		–20	8

2	–12 ÷ 4	3	–16
		–8	–3
4	15 ÷ 5	5	–3
		3	–10
6	12 ÷ –6 x 2	4	–6
		–4	6

Calculate the following.

7 –6 x 2 = ____________

8 –10 ÷ –5 = ____________

9 –3 x –7 = ____________

10 18 ÷ –6 = ____________

11 9 x –1 = ____________

12 –12 ÷ –3 = ____________

13 –8 ÷ 4 x –1 = ____________

14 6 x –1 ÷ –2 = ____________

Fill in the gaps in order to complete correct calculations.

15 3 x ☐ = –15

16 –9 x ☐ = –18

17 ☐ ÷ –5 = 4

18 –44 ÷ ☐ = 11

ISBN: 9780170447379

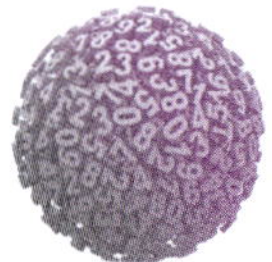

Types of numbers

Multiples

- Multiples of a number are the results of multiplying the number by another number.

Examples: The multiples of **2** are: **2**, **4**, **6**, **8**, **10**, …
The multiples of **5** are: **5**, **10**, **15**, **20**, …

These are the answers from the times tables.

1 Complete the table.

Number	First five multiples
2	2, 4, 6, 8, 10
3	
6	
4	
10	
9	
11	
7	
20	
5	
1	
8	

2 Complete the table by stating if these are true or false.

Statement	True or False
12 is a multiple of 4	
21 is a multiple of 7	
15 is a multiple of 2	
7 is a multiple of 1	
11 is a multiple of 33	
19 is a multiple of 6	
24 is a multiple of 3	
40 is a multiple of 5	
15 is a multiple of 30	
99 is a multiple of 3	
72 is a multiple of 12	
239 is a multiple of 3	

3 Multiples maze
Highlight all the multiples of 6 to get from the start to the finish of the maze. You may move horizontally or vertically but not diagonally.

Start

66	42	16	62	78	54	30
82	12	64	72	60	22	114
18	108	26	132	28	38	126
48	46	84	36	104	10	90
96	24	120	14	76	68	**102**

Finish

ISBN: 9780170447379

Lowest common multiple (LCM)

The lowest common multiple of two numbers is the **smallest multiple** of **both** numbers.

Example: The multiples of **2** are 2, 4, **6**, 8, 10, **12**, …
The multiples of **3** are 3, **6**, 9, **12**, 15, …
The multiples they have in **common** (are on both lists) are **6**, **12**, …
The **lowest common multiple** of **2** and **3** is **6**.

Write enough multiples of these numbers in order to highlight common ones, and identify the lowest.

4 Multiples of 3: ______________________
Multiples of 4: ______________________
The lowest common multiple of 3 and 4 is: __________

5 Multiples of 2: ______________________
Multiples of 5: ______________________
The lowest common multiple of 2 and 5 is: __________

6 Multiples of 6: ______________________
Multiples of 8: ______________________
The lowest common multiple of 6 and 8 is: __________

7 Multiples of 3: ______________________
Multiples of 5: ______________________
The lowest common multiple of 3 and 5 is: __________

8 Multiples of 6: ______________________
Multiples of 15: ______________________
The lowest common multiple of 6 and 15 is: __________

9 Multiples of 10: ______________________
Multiples of 12: ______________________
The lowest common multiple of 10 and 12 is: __________

10 Jo can bike around the velodrome in 4 minutes, Chrystal can bike round it in 6 minutes. If they start at the same time, how long will it take for them complete a lap together?

____

____

ISBN: 9780170447379

Factors

- Factors of a number are all the numbers that **divide** into it exactly.

Example: The factors of **8** are: **1**, **2**, **4**, 8.
The factors of **12** are: **1**, **2**, 3, **4**, 6, 12.

- The **common factors** of two numbers are those that are **factors of both**.

Example: The common factors of **8** and **12** are **1**, **2** and **4** because they are on both lists.

1 Complete the table.

Number	Factors
10	1, 2, 5, 10
14	
18	
21	
9	
15	
6	
20	
11	
30	
24	
100	

2 Complete the table by stating if these are true or false.

Statement	True or False
2 is a factor of 23	
1 is a factor of 19	
5 is a factor of 34	
3 is a factor of 27	
4 is a factor of 34	
2 is a factor of 13	
9 is a factor of 63	
7 is a factor of 35	
8 is a factor of 4	
4 is a factor of 28	
3 is a factor of 333	
0 is a factor of 15	

3 Factors maze
Highlight all the factors of 60 to get from the start to the finish of the maze. You may move horizontally or vertically but not diagonally.

Start

10	7	25	9	17	22	39
5	15	1	6	13	42	27
14	23	8	2	32	38	19
11	24	31	30	10	12	33
21	0	45	16	28	4	**60**

Finish

ISBN: 9780170447379

Highest common factor (HCF)

- The highest common factor of two numbers is the **largest** common factor of **both** numbers.

Example: The factors of **12** are **1**, **2**, 3, **4**, 6, 12.
The factors of **16** are **1**, **2**, **4**, 8, 16.
The factors they have in **common** are **1**, **2** and **4**.
The **highest common factor** of **12** and **16** is **4**.

Write all the factors of these numbers, highlight the common ones and then identify the highest.

4 Factors of 15: ______
Factors of 20: ______
The highest common factor of 15 and 20 is: ______

5 Factors of 6: ______
Factors of 12: ______
The highest common factor of 6 and 12 is: ______

6 Factors of 10: ______
Factors of 24: ______
The highest common factor of 10 and 24 is: ______

7 Factors of 30: ______
Factors of 40: ______
The highest common factor of 30 and 40 is: ______

8 Factors of 11: ______
Factors of 22: ______
The highest common factor of 11 and 22 is: ______

9 Factors of 27: ______
Factors of 63: ______
The highest common factor of 27 and 63 is: ______

10 A Physical Education teacher wants to split her class of 16 girls and 8 boys into groups with the same number of girls and the same number of boys in each. There should be no one left out. What are some options she has?

She could have ______ groups with ______ girls and ______ boys in each group.

She could have ______ groups with ______ girls and ______ boys in each group.

She could have ______ groups with ______ girls and ______ boys in each group.

ISBN: 9780170447379

Prime numbers

- A prime number has **exactly two factors**: 1 and itself.

Examples: 2 **is** a prime number because it has exactly **two** factors: **1** and **2**.
7 **is** a prime number because it has exactly **two** factors: **1** and **7**.
6 **is not** a prime number because it has **four** factors: **1**, **2**, **3** and **6**.

Note: 1 **is not** a prime number because it has only **one** factor: **1**.

1 Highlight the prime numbers between 1 and 40. (Hint: You should find twelve.)

1	2	3	4	5	6	7	8	9	10
11	12	13	14	15	16	17	18	19	20
21	22	23	24	25	26	27	28	29	30
31	32	33	34	35	36	37	38	39	40

2 What is the next prime number after 40? ____________________

3 Are all prime numbers odd? Give a reason for your answer.

____

____

4 Can you find three different sets of prime numbers that add to 24?

☐ + ☐ = 24

☐ + ☐ = 24

☐ + ☐ = 24

ISBN: 9780170447379

Prime factors

- All non-prime numbers can be written as products of prime factors.
- Prime numbers and their factors are very important in cryptography (writing and using codes), especially for use in cyber security.

Examples:

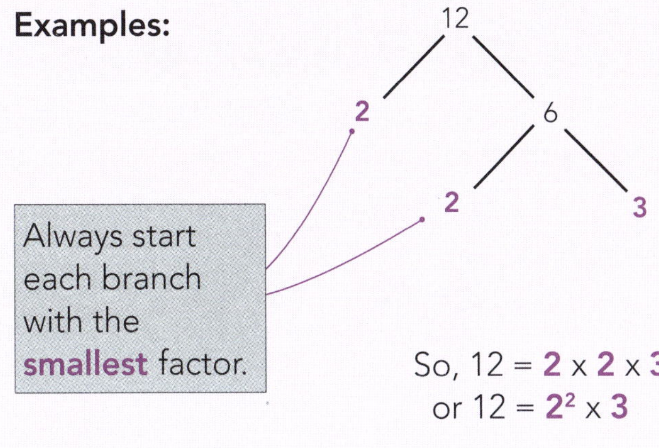

So, $12 = 2 \times 2 \times 3$
or $12 = 2^2 \times 3$

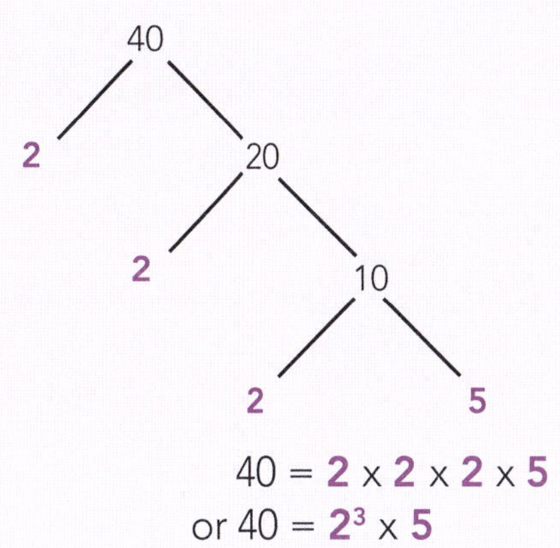

$40 = 2 \times 2 \times 2 \times 5$
or $40 = 2^3 \times 5$

Complete these prime factor trees.

5

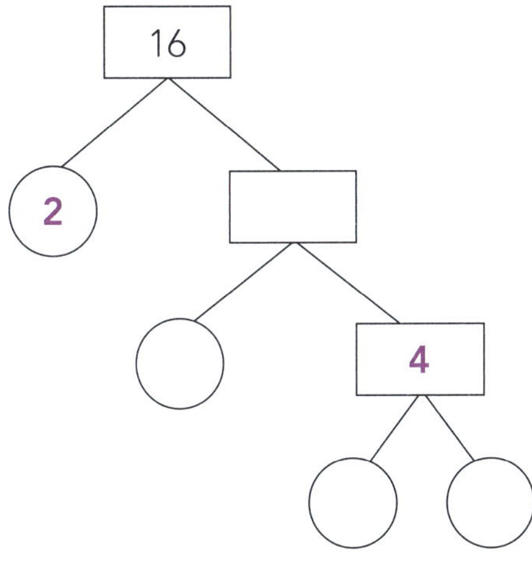

16 = ____________________

6

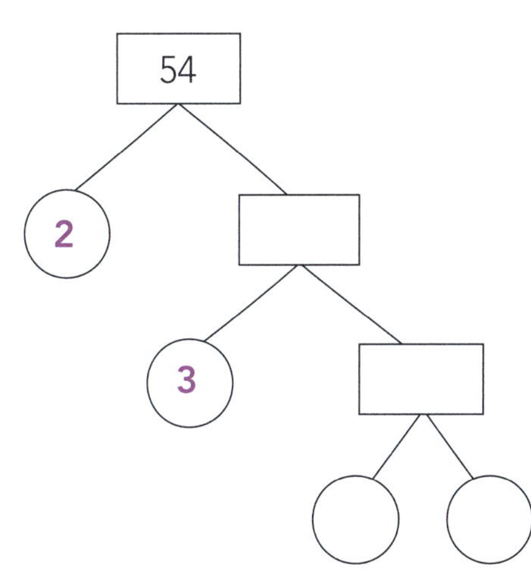

54 = ____________________

7

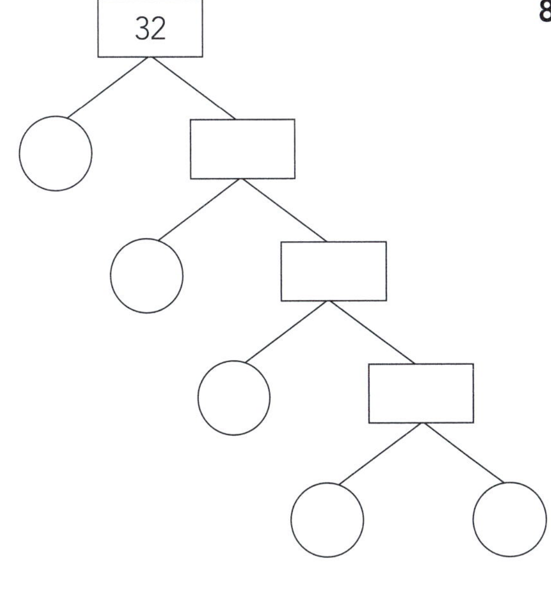

32 = ____________________

8

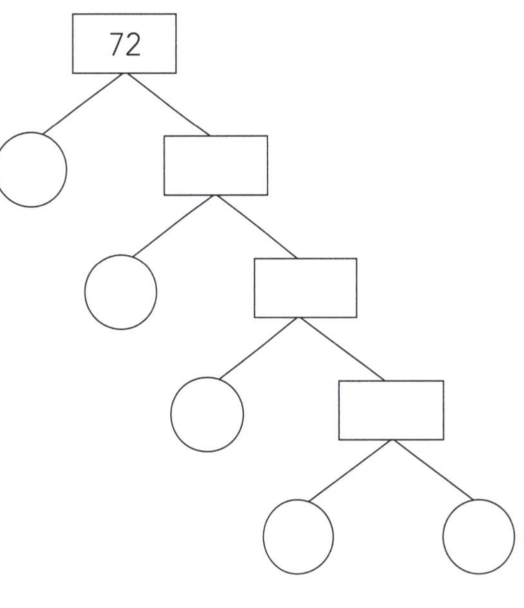

72 = ____________________

ISBN: 9780170447379

9

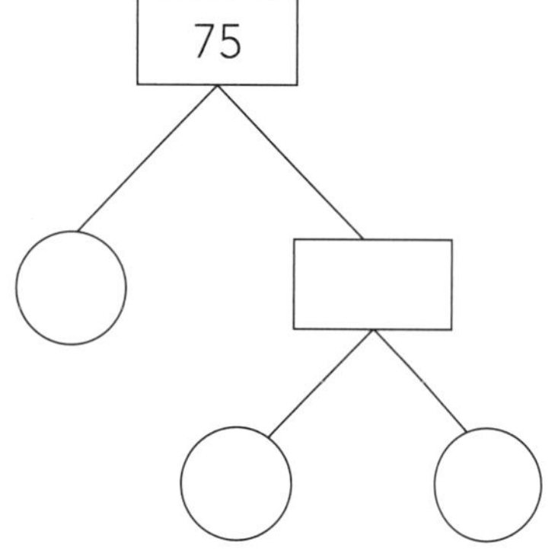

75 = ____________________

10

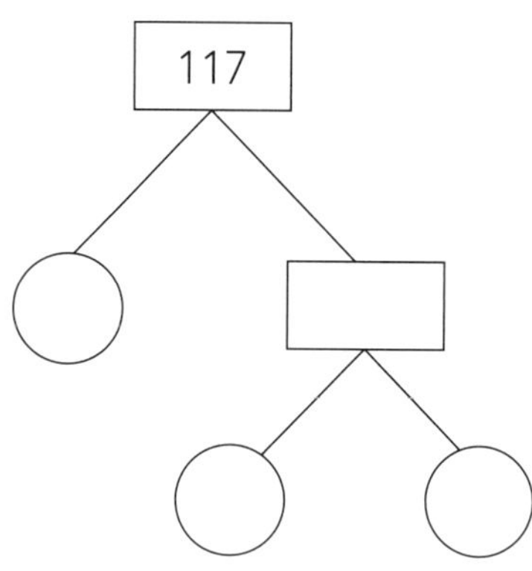

117 = ____________________

11

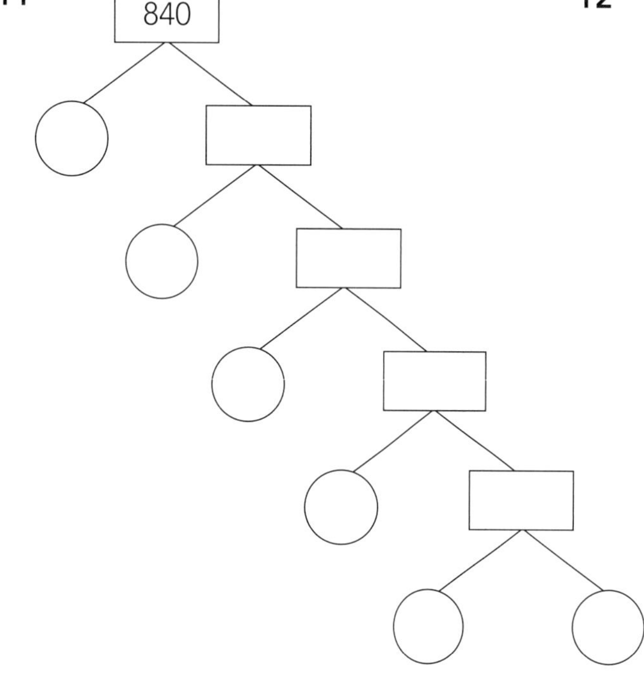

840 = ____________________

12

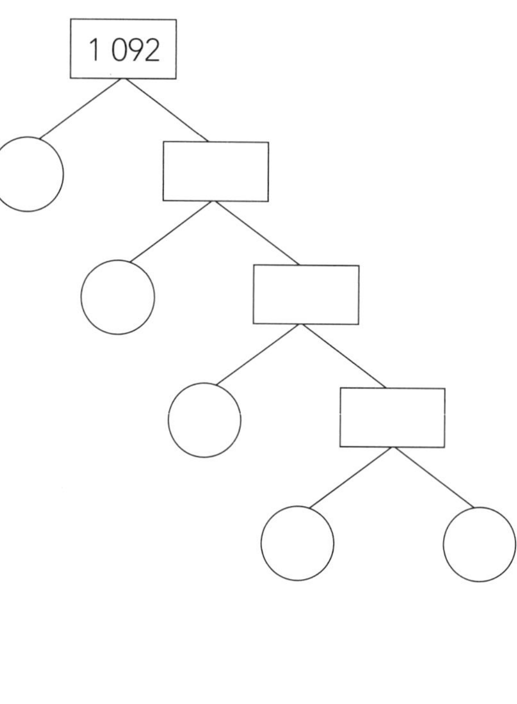

1 092 = ____________________

Draw your own factor trees for these.

13 140

140 = ____________________

14 147

147 = ____________________

 ISBN: 9780170447379

Square numbers

- A square number is a product (x) of two equal counting numbers (counting numbers are 1, 2, 3, …).
- Square numbers can be drawn as a square pattern of dots.

Examples: 9 **is** a square number because it is a product of 3 and 3, and it equals **3^2**.

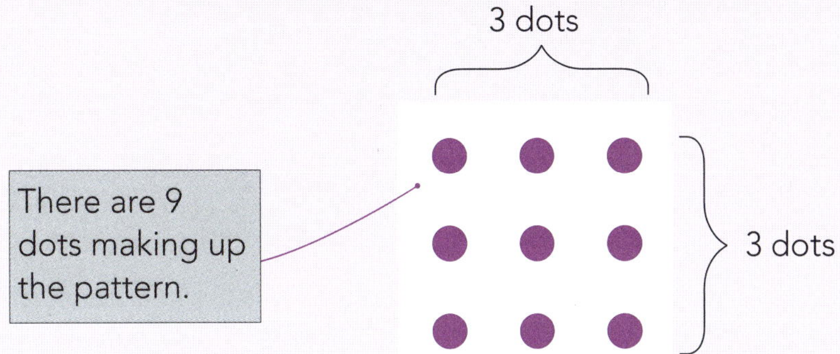

6 **is not** a square number because it cannot be written as a product of two equal numbers. Nor can 6 dots be drawn in a square.

1 Complete the patterns and fill in the missing numbers.

Square number	Picture	Notation
1		1^2
4	● ● ● ●	
		3^2
	● ● ● ● ● ● ● ● ● ● ● ● ● ● ● ●	4^2
25		
		6^2

ISBN: 9780170447379

Powers

- Powers are used to indicate how many times a number (the base) is multiplied by itself.

The **2** is called the **base**.

The **4** is known as the **power** or the **exponent** or the **index**.

Example: $2^4 = 2 \times 2 \times 2 \times 2$
$= 16$

- When a power is **2**, we say the number is **squared**, e.g. 5^2 means five **squared** (= 25).
- When a power is **3**, we say the number is **cubed**, e.g. 2^3 means two **cubed** (= 8).
- **Important:** **anything^1 = itself** e.g. $7^1 = 7$
  anything^0 = 1 e.g. $7^0 = 1$

The power indicates how many times you need to multiply.

Examples: $7^2 = 7 \times 7$
$= 49$

$3^4 = 3 \times 3 \times 3 \times 3$
$= 81$

Finding powers on your calculator

- Powers of numbers can get really big, so knowing how to find them on your calculator is **very** useful.

For squares: use a button that looks like this:  e.g. show that $14^2 = 196$.

For cubes: use a button that looks like this:  e.g. show that $7^3 = 343$.

For all other powers: use a button that looks like this:  or  or 
e.g. show that $2^7 = 128$.

Write the following as powers.

1 $4 \times 4 \times 4 \times 4 \times 4$ = ____________

2 6×6 = ____________

3 $5 \times 5 \times 5$ = ____________

4 $9 \times 9 \times 9 \times 9$ = ____________

5 8 = ____________

6 $3 \times 3 \times 3$ = ____________

7 2×2 = ____________

8 1 = ____________

ISBN: 9780170447379

Write out what the following mean and then calculate that.

9 $2^5 = 2 \times 2 \times 2 \times 2 \times 2 =$ ______ **10** $4^3 =$ ______

11 $9^2 =$ ______ **12** $8^4 =$ ______

13 $7^3 =$ ______ **14** $10^1 =$ ______

15 $5^6 =$ ______ **16** $6^0 =$ ______

17 $3^5 =$ ______ **18** $3^2 \times 3^3 =$ ______

19 Are your last two answers the same? ______

What number should go in the box: $3^2 \times 3^3 = 3^{\square}$? ______

Use your calculator to find the values of the following.

20 $5^2 + 2^3 =$ ______ **21** $4^5 - 3^2 =$ ______

22 $2^2 \times 6^2 =$ ______ **23** $8^2 \div 4^2 =$ ______

24 $\frac{6^3}{3^3} =$ ______ **25** $10^3 + 5^2 - 2^2 =$ ______

26 $0.3^2 =$ ______ **27** $2^{-1} =$ ______

Puzzle

Match the answers in the boxes to each of the questions below. Use your calculator to help you.

125	$\frac{1}{5}$	1	625	5
–125	3 125	15 625	25	$\frac{1}{25}$

28 $5^2 =$ ______ **29** $25^2 =$ ______

30 $(-5)^3 =$ ______ **31** $5^3 =$ ______

32 $5^{-1} =$ ______ **33** $5^1 =$ ______

34 $5^0 =$ ______ **35** $25^3 =$ ______

36 $5^5 =$ ______ **37** $25^{-1} =$ ______

ISBN: 9780170447379

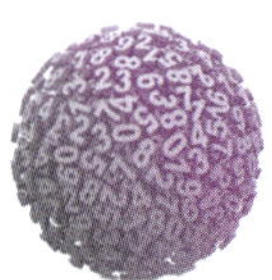

Roots

- Finding a root is the opposite of finding a power.
- The **square root** is written as $\sqrt{}$. You do not need to write $\sqrt[2]{}$.

  e.g. $\sqrt{9} = \sqrt{3 \times 3}$
  $= 3$
- The **cube root** is written as $\sqrt[3]{}$.

  e.g. $\sqrt[3]{8} = \sqrt[3]{2 \times 2 \times 2}$
  $= 2$
- The **fourth root** is written $\sqrt[4]{}$, the **fifth root** is written as $\sqrt[5]{}$, etc.

  e.g. $\sqrt[5]{32} = \sqrt[5]{2 \times 2 \times 2 \times 2 \times 2}$
  $= 2$

You can do this on your calculator with either 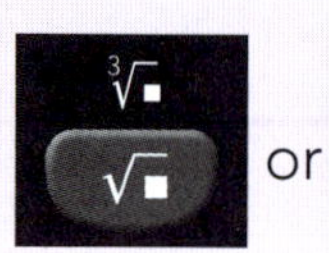 or .

Find the following roots.

1 $\sqrt{9} =$ ________________ **2** $\sqrt{25} =$ ________________

3 $\sqrt{49} =$ ________________ **4** $\sqrt{81} =$ ________________

5 $\sqrt[3]{8} =$ ________________ **6** $\sqrt[3]{216} =$ ________________

7 $\sqrt[3]{1\,000} =$ ________________ **8** $\sqrt[4]{1\,296} =$ ________________

9 $\sqrt[5]{32} =$ ________________ **10** $\sqrt[6]{729} =$ ________________

11 $\sqrt[7]{128} =$ ________________ **12** $\sqrt{0.25} =$ ________________

ISBN: 9780170447379

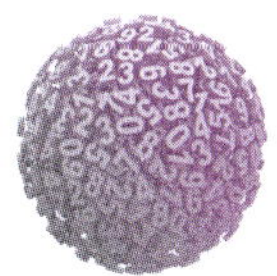

Order of operations

- **BEDMAS** helps us to remember the order of operations.
- If you have several division signs or several multiplication signs, work from left to right.
- The horizontal division symbol in a fraction means you must bracket the numerator and bracket the denominator.

Fill in the table below and use it to help you remember the order to use in calculations:

B	
E	
D	
M	
A	
S	

Remember: when there is more than one of these, work from left to right.

If there is no sign between two values, it means you multiply them.

Examples:

1 $10 - 8 \div 2^2$ — Exponents first

$= 10 - 8 \div 4$ — Division next

$= 10 - 2$ — Subtraction last

$= 8$

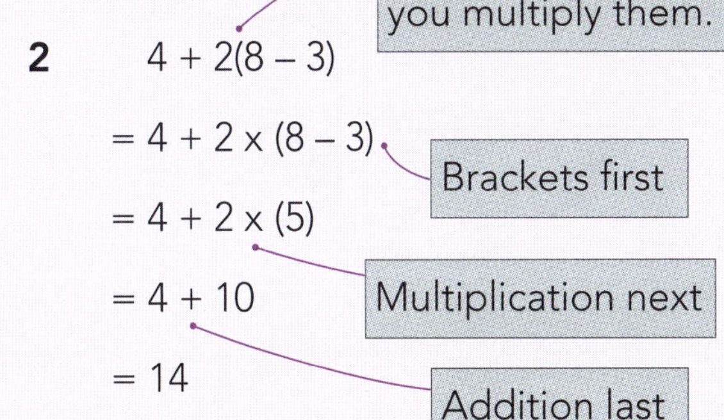

2 $4 + 2(8 - 3)$

$= 4 + 2 \times (8 - 3)$ — Brackets first

$= 4 + 2 \times (5)$ — Multiplication next

$= 4 + 10$ — Addition last

$= 14$

Highlight the correct answer for each of the following.

1	$10 - 3 \times 2$	6	14
		4	17
3	$6 + 2^2$	10	64
		4	2
5	$1 + (5 - 1)^2$	17	16
		6	5
7	$6 \div 3(1 + 1)$	2	1
		4	3

2	$\frac{4 + 2}{2}$	6	4
		3	1
4	$8 + 2(6 - 1)$	−2	18
		50	10
6	$18 - (6 - (2 + 1))^2$	3	21
		9	1
8	$80 - 9^2 + 1$	10	0
		5	2

ISBN: 9780170447379

Using BEDMAS, calculate the following.

9 $-3 + 6 \times 2 =$ ______________

10 $(-3 + 6) \times 2 =$ ______________

11 $3 + 2^2 =$ ______________

12 $(3 + 2)^2 =$ ______________

13 $12 \times -3 \div -2 =$ ______________

14 $12 \div -3 \times 2 =$ ______________

15 $\dfrac{5 + 3^2}{2} =$ ______________

16 $10 - 3 \times 2 + 2 =$ ______________

17 $(4 + 2 \times 3) \div 5 =$ ______________

18 $\dfrac{28}{15 - 2^2 \times 2} =$ ______________

Don't forget to use BEDMAS for these puzzles.

19 If:

+ + = 18

+ − = 10

+ x = ______________

then:

= ______________

= ______________

20 If:

+ + = 12

+ ÷ = 6

(−) x = ______________

then:

= ______________

= ______________

 ISBN: 9780170447379

Words to calculations

Match the calculations with the stories below, and calculate the answer to each. You will not need to use all of these calculations.

$(14 - 4) \times 2$	$\frac{14}{2} + 4$	$(14 \times 2) - 4$	$14 + 2 - 4$
$14 - 2 + 4$	$14 \div 4 - 2$	$(14 + 4) \div 2$	$\frac{14 - 4}{2}$
$14 \times (2 + 2)$	$14 \times 4 - 2$	$(14 + 4) \times 2$	$14 \times (2 - 4)$
$\frac{14 - 2}{4}$	$((14 \times 2) + 2) \div 2$	$14 \times (2 + 4) \times 2$	$(14 + 2) \div 4$

	Story	Calculation	Solution
1	Hank and Luke bought their mother some flowers that cost $14 and a card for $4. If they shared the cost equally, how much did each pay?	________	$ ______
2	Two friends went to the movies; their tickets each cost $14 and they shared some $2 popcorn. How much did it cost each friend?	________	$ ______
3	Oscar's hens laid 14 eggs on Saturday, but he accidentally broke 2 eggs. On Sunday they laid 4 more. How many eggs does Oscar have left to sell?	________	______
4	Charlie was given $14 for cleaning the car, but she paid her brother the $4 she owed him. She then spent half. How much money did Charlie have left?	________	$ ______
5	Gus found $14 in the street and gave his sister half. Gus then added it to his wallet, which already had $4 in it. How much money does Gus have in his wallet?	________	$ ______
6	On Thursday, Sarah sold 14 of her artworks for $2 each. It cost her $4 to rent the stall. How much money did she make?	________	$ ______
7	A family of two adults and two children went to the zoo. It cost the adults $14 each and children $4 each. How much did it cost the family to enter the zoo?	________	$ ______
8	Bernie spent $2 of her $14. She shared the rest equally between her four siblings. How much did each sibling get?	________	$ ______

ISBN: 9780170447379

Using your calculator

Do the calculations on the next page using your calculator, then turn your calculator upside down and add the word to the story below. Be careful to check that it makes sense.

Example: $195^2 + 51 = 38076$, upside down this spells GLOBE.

The muster

1 ______________ and 2 ______________ sat on the 3 ______________ 4 ______________ waiting for the 5 ______________ to 6 ______________. The sun was going down. It would be hard to 7 ______________ soon. 8 ______________ leg kicked out at the 9 ______________, shaking his boot 10 ______________. He was desperate to lie down and sleep but felt 11 ______________ with hunger, the 12 ______________ rising up. The pan began to 13 ______________ as 14 ______________ put the 15 ______________ in. 16 ______________ oozed out of the 17 ______________ cut. He cracked the 18 ______________ and they began to 19 ______________ over as they cooked. There was nothing else. 20 ______________ began to 21 ______________ the food. 22 ______________ passed 23 ______________ the plate. They began to 24 ______________ the food down. 25 ______________ would 26 ______________ by cleaning the plates. They lay down to sleep. The 27 ______________ of his feet hurt, his 28 ______________ ached, his arm itched where he had been stung by a 29 ______________ but he was not hungry any more. They had the steers down. The muster was nearly done.

ISBN: 9780170447379

1 $7 \times 2^3 \times (5 \times 1\,138 + 3)$

2 $\frac{1\,059}{3} \times \sqrt{8\,100}$

3 $2((1 + 2) + 3) \times 52 - 6$

4 $\sqrt{36} \times \frac{1\,000}{10} - -7$

5 $\frac{7^2}{3.5} \times (6^2 \times \sqrt{9} \times 3\,517 + 1)$

6 $\sqrt{16}\left(\frac{900}{30} \times 5.9 \times 10 + 7\right)$

7 $2^2(17 - 0.25) \times \sqrt{25}$

8 $(((2 + 1) + 2) + 1) \times \frac{2\,420}{2.5}$

9 $7^2 \times (5^3 + (2^2 \times \sqrt{25}))$

10 $\sqrt[3]{((1.25 \times 10^{11}) + 1)} \times \sqrt{49} + 7$

11 $\frac{(16^2 + 1) \times 30}{\sqrt{100}}$

12 $4^{7-1} - (3 \times (6 + 1)) \times \frac{36}{2}$

13 $\sqrt{25}(40 \times 1\,861 + 3)$

14 $12(3^4 \times 2^5) + 666$

15 $7 \times \sqrt{10\,000} + \sqrt[3]{27} \times 11$

16 $10(3^4 - \sqrt{100})$

17 $\frac{1\,068}{89} \times (4^2 \times \frac{120}{\sqrt{9}} + 3)$

18 $(8 \times 10^2 + 9) \times \sqrt[3]{(7 \times 49)}$

19 $300^2 - 185^2 - 25^2 - 8^2 - 10$

20 $10^2 \times \frac{1}{2} \times \frac{2\,118}{\sqrt{9}} - 706 \times \sqrt[3]{125}$

21 $\frac{10 \times (94^2 + 4^2 + 13^2 + 3^1)}{6 \times 2^2}$

22 $2(25^3 + 46) + 42.8 \times 10$

23 $2^2(2^2 + 3) \times (\sqrt{4} \times \sqrt{100} \times 569 + 6)$

24 $\frac{222}{\sqrt{9}} \times (71^2 + 78)$

25 $((10^2\,(4^2 + 1) \div 2) - 42)$

26 $\frac{50^4 - (20^2 \times 250 - 260)}{17}$

27 $\frac{575}{5} \times ((\sqrt[3]{125} \times 2^2 - 2)(2 \times 13) - 1)$

28 $76^2 - (6^2 \times \sqrt{9} + 31)$

29 $3^6 - 7^3 - (\sqrt{36} \times 2^2) + 23$

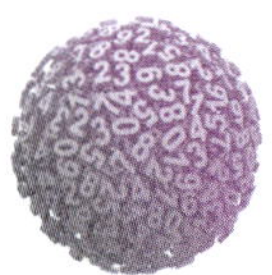

Mixing it up

1 List the factors of 18.

2 Is 93 a multiple of 3? Explain your answer.

3 Use BEDMAS to calculate the following.

a $2 \times (19 + 1) \div 2^2 =$ ________

b $\frac{3^3 - 6}{(2 + 1)} =$ ________

4 Calculate these.

a $9 - -1 + -4 =$ ________

b $24 \div -6 \times -2 =$ ________

5 Fill in the boxes with the correct integers.

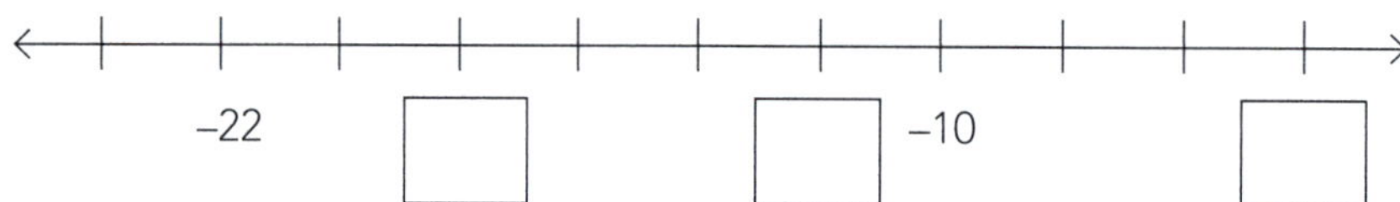

6 **a** Is 63 a prime number? How do you know?

b Complete this prime factorisation tree.

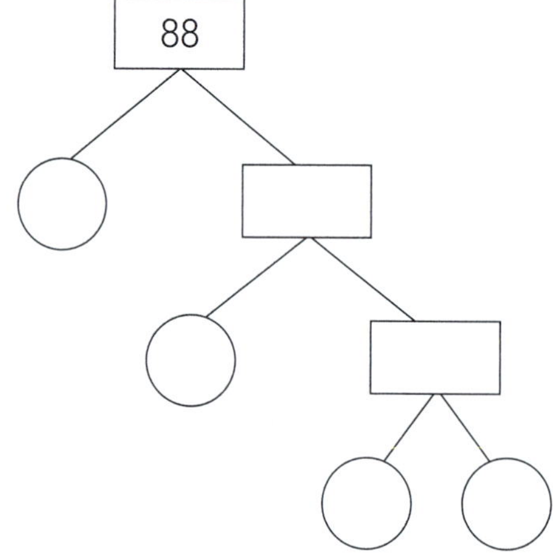

c What is the only even prime number?

Calculate these.

7 **a** $\sqrt{64} =$ ________

b $8^2 =$ ________

8 What is the seventh square number?

9 $\frac{3^2 \times (\sqrt{81} + 3^1)}{18} =$ ________

 ISBN: 9780170447379

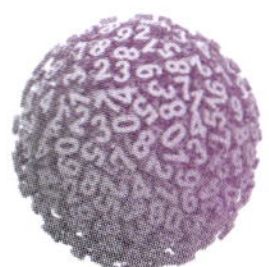

Fractions

Shading fractions

- Fractions are a way of writing numbers or parts of numbers.

Examples:

1 **One** part of the **three** is shaded:

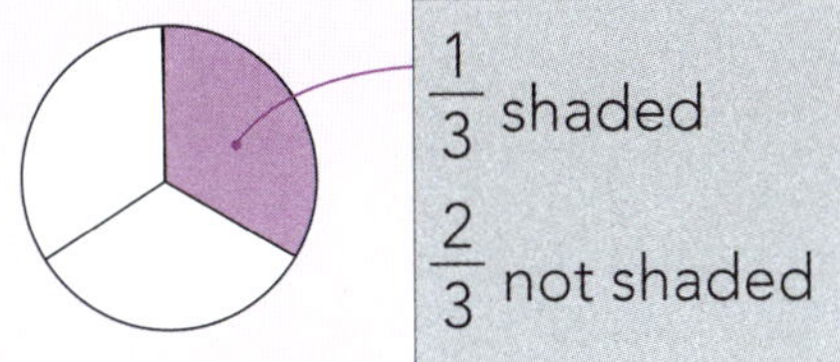

2 **Three** parts out of **eight** are shaded:

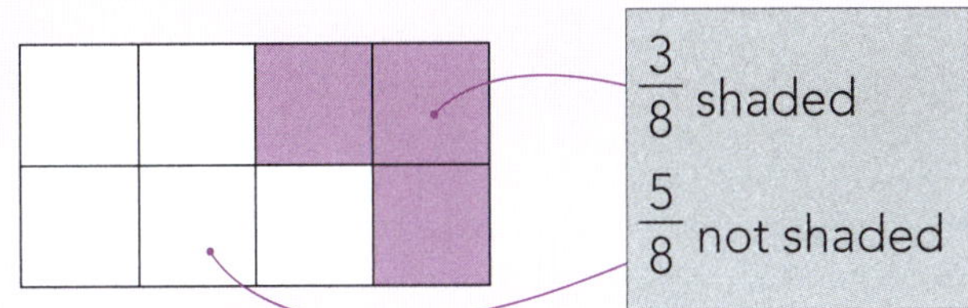

What fractions of these diagrams are shaded and not shaded?

1

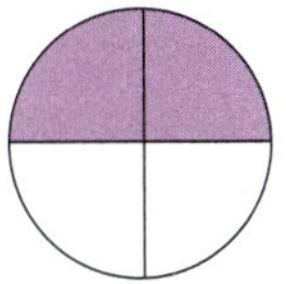

Shaded ______

Not shaded ______

2

Shaded ______

Not shaded ______

3

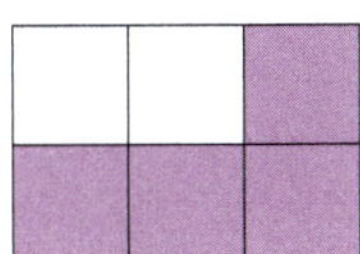

Shaded ______

Not shaded ______

4

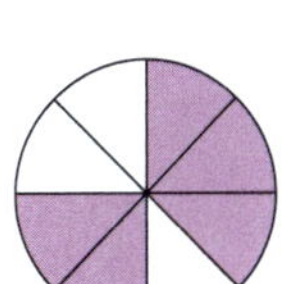

Shaded ______

Not shaded ______

5

Shaded ______

Not shaded ______

6

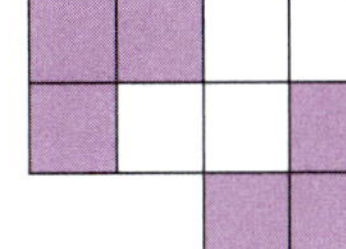

Shaded ______

Not shaded ______

7

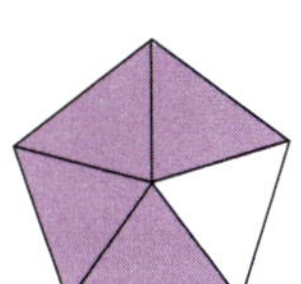

Shaded ______

Not shaded ______

8

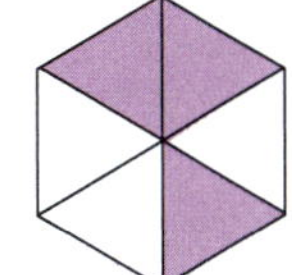

Shaded ______

Not shaded ______

9

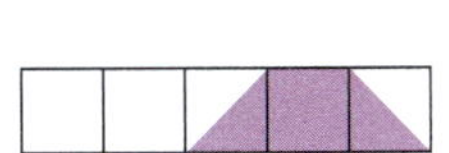

Shaded ______

Not shaded ______

10

Shaded ______

Not shaded ______

11 What do you notice when you add each pair of fractions?

____

ISBN: 9780170447379

Shade the diagram to match the fraction.

12

$\frac{3}{4}$

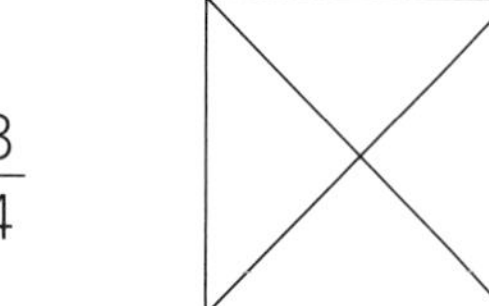

13

$\frac{3}{8}$

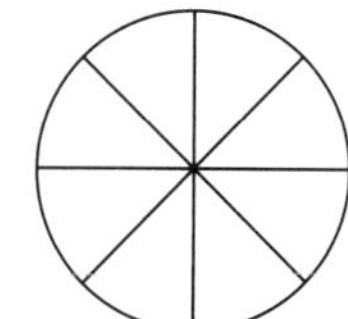

14

$\frac{2}{6}$

15

$\frac{4}{5}$

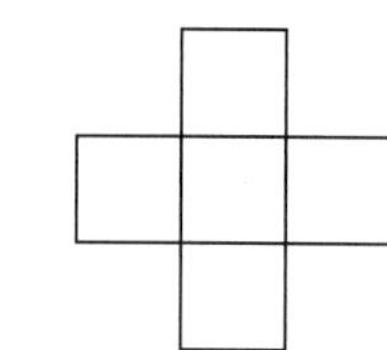

16

$\frac{1}{4}$

17

$\frac{3}{10}$

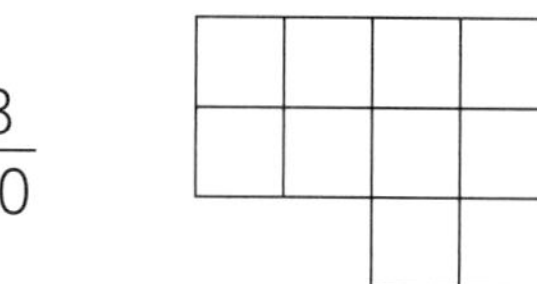

18

$\frac{5}{7}$

19

$\frac{5}{8}$

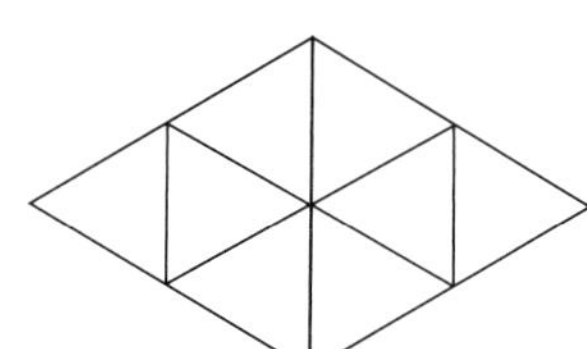

20

$\frac{8}{9}$

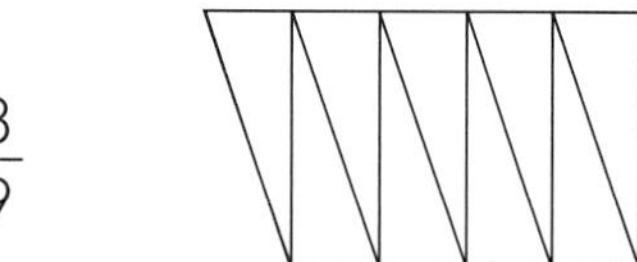

21

$\frac{3}{5}$

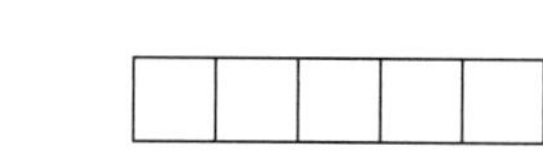

22

$\frac{1}{3}$

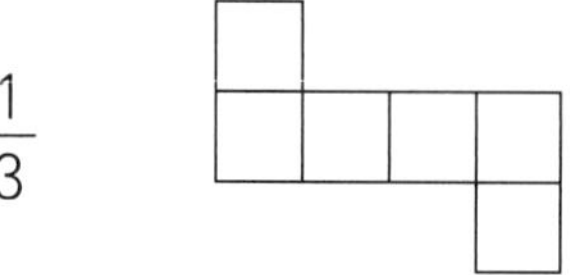

23

$\frac{3}{4}$

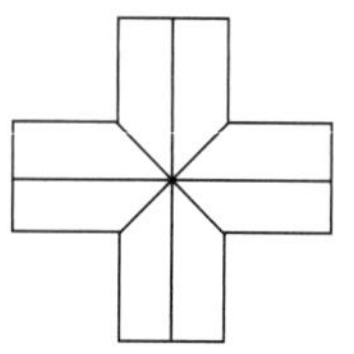

24

$\frac{2}{8}$

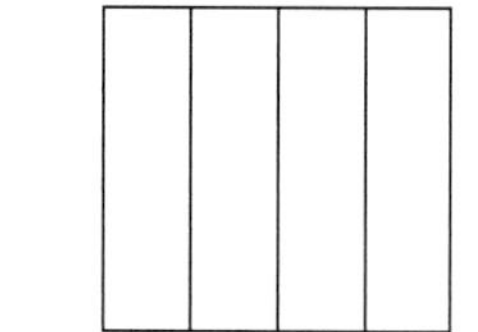

25

$\frac{2}{6}$

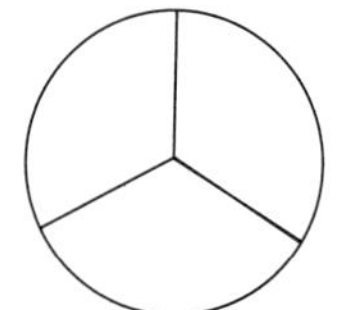

 ISBN: 9780170447379

Numerators and denominators

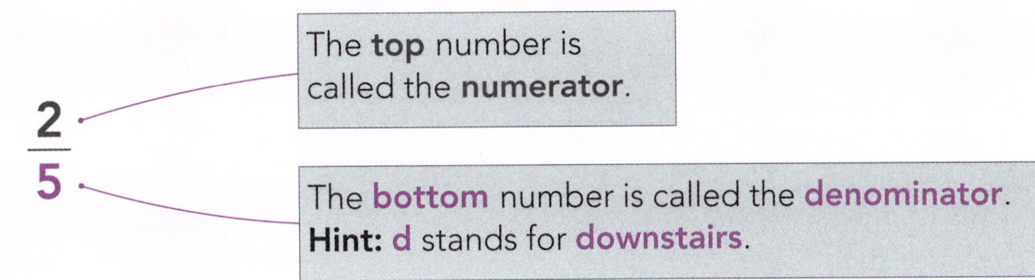

Shade the fraction represented in each diagram and cross out the word to make a true statement.

1

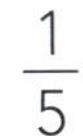

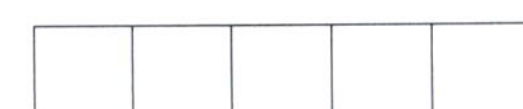

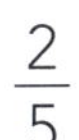

When the **numerator** increases, the size of the shaded section **increases/decreases**.

2

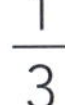

$\frac{1}{4}$

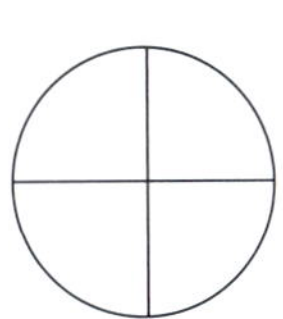

When the **denominator** increases, the size of the shaded section **increases/decreases**.

Complete the fractions so they match the diagrams, then highlight the larger one.

3

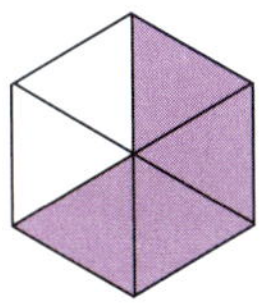

$\frac{\quad}{6}$ $\frac{\quad}{6}$

4

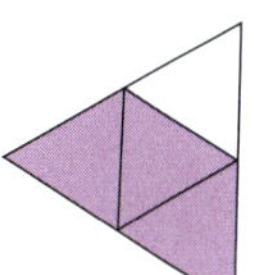

$\frac{\quad}{4}$ $\frac{\quad}{4}$

5

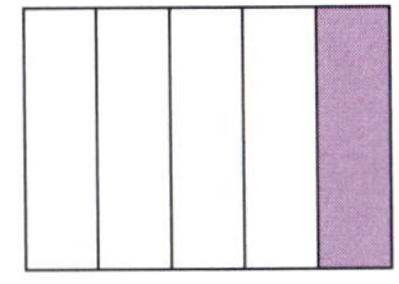

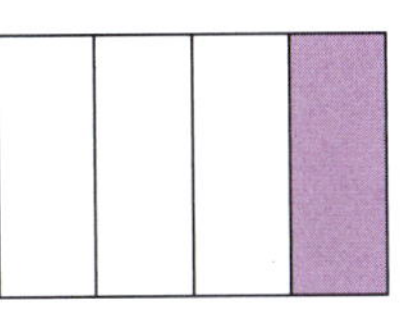

$\frac{1}{\quad}$ $\frac{1}{\quad}$

6

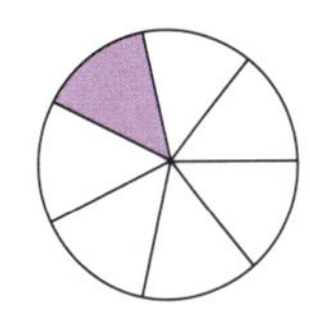

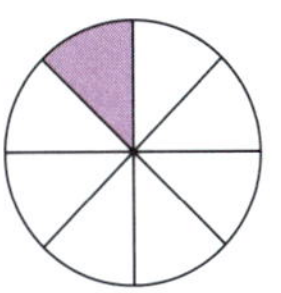

$\frac{1}{\quad}$ $\frac{1}{\quad}$

ISBN: 9780170447379

Circle or highlight which fraction is larger.

7 $\frac{1}{5}$ $\frac{2}{5}$

8 $\frac{1}{7}$ $\frac{1}{5}$

9 $\frac{9}{10}$ $\frac{7}{10}$

10 $\frac{3}{9}$ $\frac{3}{8}$

11 **a** Shade the diagrams so they match the fractions.

$\frac{1}{6}$ 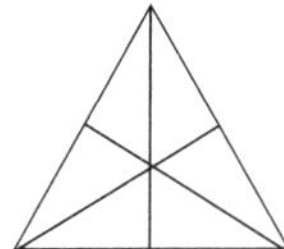
$\frac{4}{6}$ 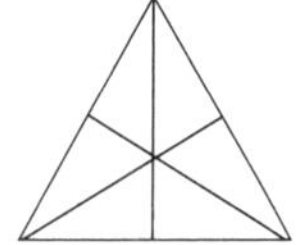
$\frac{2}{6}$ 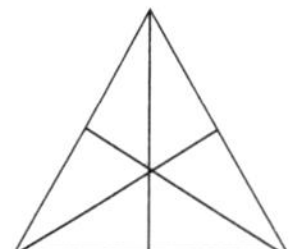
$\frac{5}{6}$ 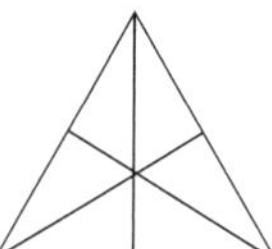
$\frac{6}{6}$ 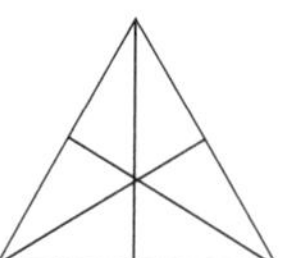
$\frac{3}{6}$ 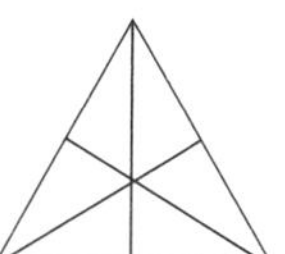

b Write the fractions in ascending order.

Smallest			$\frac{3}{6}$				Largest

12 **a** Shade the diagrams so they match the fractions.

$\frac{1}{5}$ 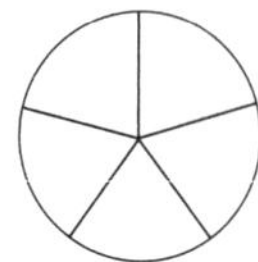
$\frac{1}{1}$ 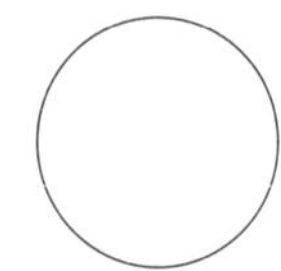
$\frac{1}{3}$ 
$\frac{1}{6}$ 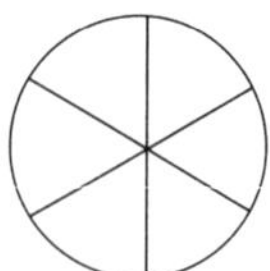
$\frac{1}{4}$ 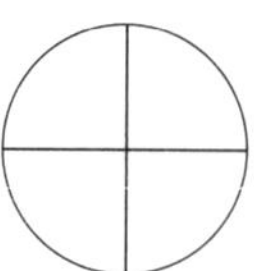
$\frac{1}{2}$ 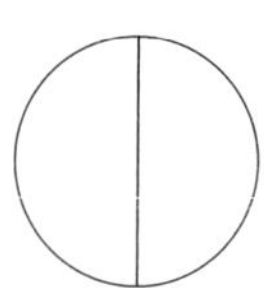

b Write the fractions in ascending order.

Smallest				$\frac{1}{3}$			Largest

ISBN: 9780170447379

Equivalent fractions

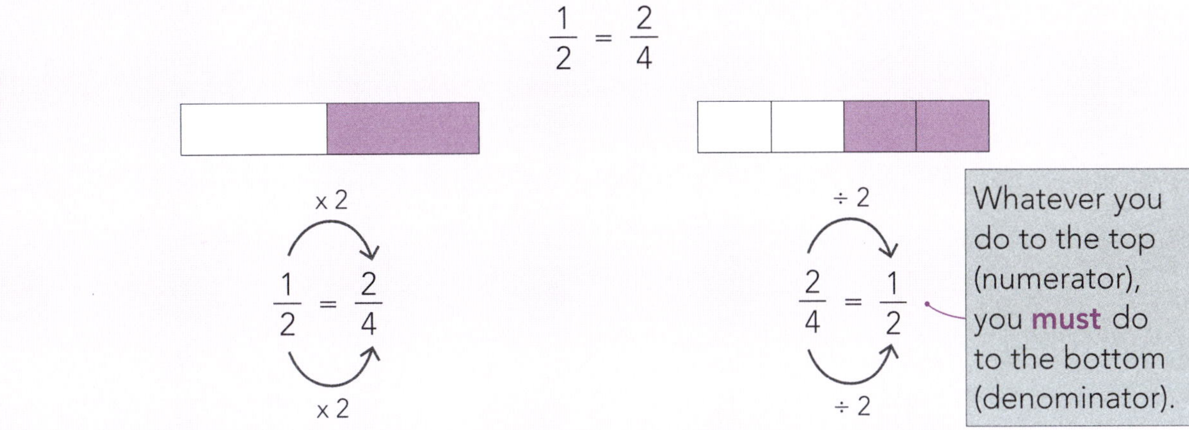

Shade the diagrams and fill the gaps to create equivalent fractions.

1

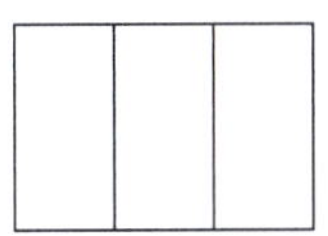

$\frac{4}{6} = \frac{\_\_}{3}$

2

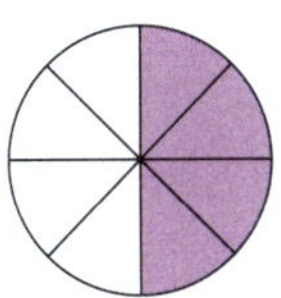

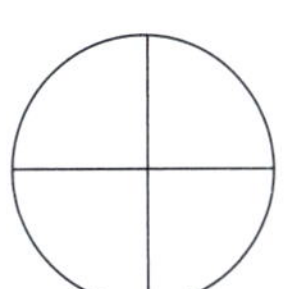

$\frac{4}{8} = \frac{\_\_}{4}$

3

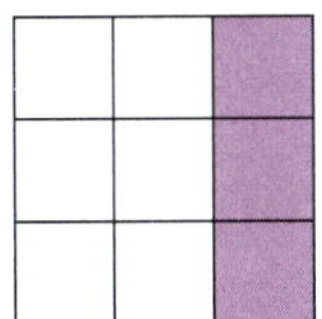

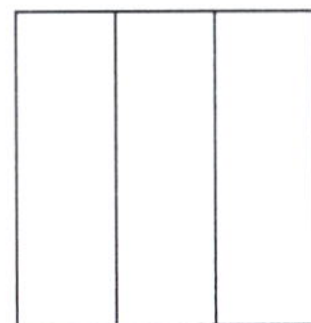

$\frac{3}{\_\_} = \frac{\_\_}{3}$

4

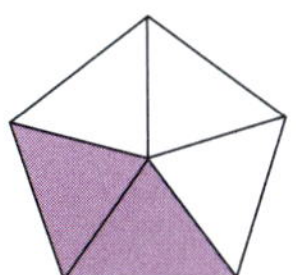

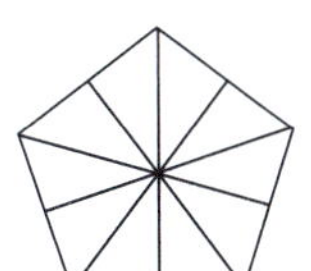

$\frac{\_\_}{5} = \frac{\_\_}{\_\_}$

5

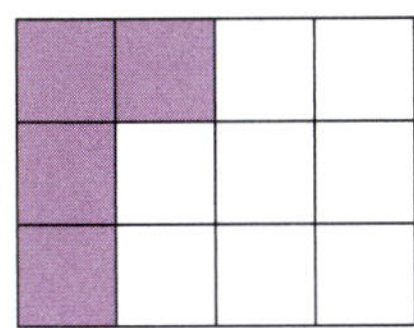

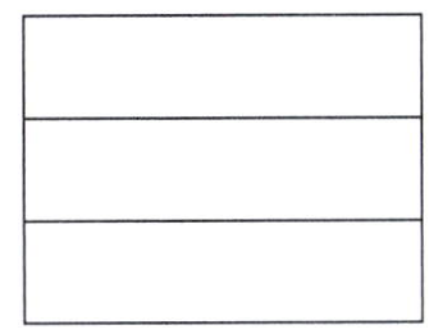

$\frac{\_\_}{\_\_} = \frac{\_\_}{\_\_}$

ISBN: 9780170447379

Fill in the gaps to create equivalent fractions.

6

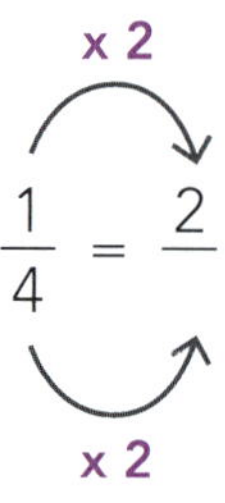

7

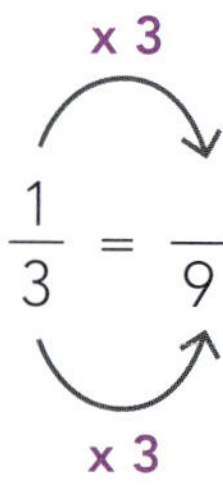

8

____

$\frac{1}{2} = \frac{4}{}$

____

9

____

$\frac{2}{3} = \frac{}{12}$

____

10

x 2

$\frac{3}{5} = \frac{}{}$

x 2

11

x 3

$\frac{1}{3} = \frac{}{}$

x 3

12

____

$\frac{2}{3} = \frac{}{15}$

____

13

____

$\frac{1}{4} = \frac{}{12}$

____

14 $\frac{1}{5} = \frac{}{10} = \frac{3}{} = \frac{}{20} = \frac{5}{} = \frac{6}{} = \frac{7}{}$

 ISBN: 9780170447379

Simplifying fractions

- Usually we want our answers in the simplest possible form.
- This means writing the fraction with the lowest possible whole numbers.
- Remember, what you do to the numerator, you must also do to the denominator.

Examples:

$$\frac{12}{20} \overset{\div 2}{=} \frac{6}{10} \overset{\div 2}{=} \frac{3}{5}$$

Halve the fraction, then halve it again.

$\div 4$

Or divide by four.

If the numbers aren't divisible by 2, then try 3 or 5. Keep going until you can't go any further.

$$\frac{6}{9} \overset{\div 3}{=} \frac{2}{3} \qquad \frac{15}{25} \overset{\div 5}{=} \frac{3}{5}$$

Fully simplify these fractions.

1 $\frac{18}{20} = \frac{9}{}$ (÷ **2**, ÷ **2**)

2 $\frac{15}{40} = \frac{}{}$ (÷ **5**, ÷ **5**)

3 $\frac{12}{21} = \frac{}{7}$ (÷ ____, ÷ ____)

4 $\frac{20}{50} = \frac{}{}$ (÷ ____, ÷ ____)

5 $\frac{15}{24} =$ ____

6 $\frac{33}{36} =$ ____

7 $\frac{3}{21} =$ ____

8 $\frac{16}{32} =$ ____

ISBN: 9780170447379

Comparing fractions

- Comparing and ordering fractions is easiest if they all have the same denominator. If they don't have the same denominator, it can be more challenging.

Example: Which is larger, $\frac{2}{3}$ or $\frac{3}{4}$?

Visually, $\frac{3}{4}$ looks larger.

Method 1: Compare pictures.

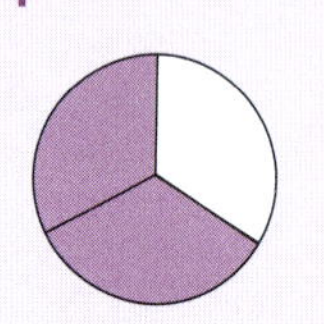

Method 2: Find the LCM of 3 and 4. Use 12 as a denominator.

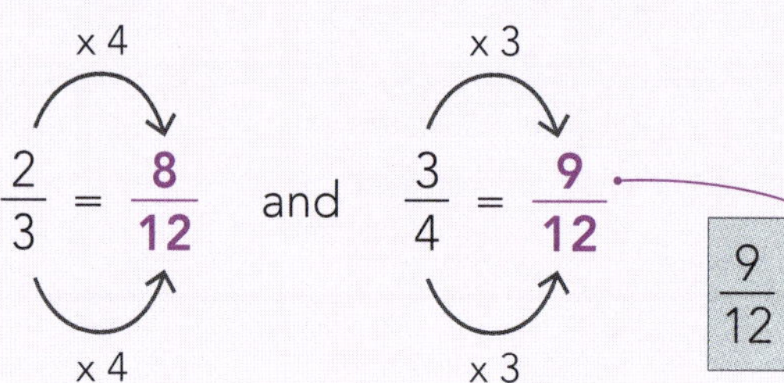

$\frac{2}{3} = \frac{8}{12}$ and $\frac{3}{4} = \frac{9}{12}$

$\frac{9}{12}$ is larger than $\frac{8}{12}$.

So, $\frac{3}{4}$ is larger than $\frac{2}{3}$.

Shade the diagrams and write which fraction is larger and which is smaller. The first one has been started for you.

1 $\frac{5}{6}$ $\frac{3}{4}$

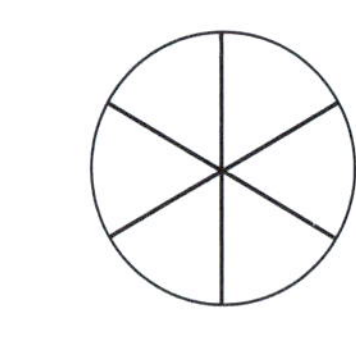
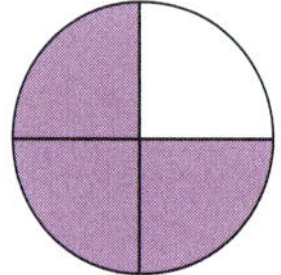

Larger ______ ______

2 $\frac{3}{7}$ $\frac{2}{5}$

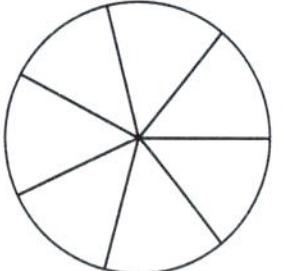

______ ______

3 $\frac{3}{5}$ $\frac{2}{3}$

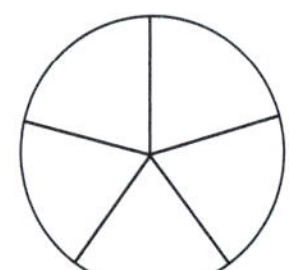

______ ______

4 $\frac{2}{9}$ $\frac{1}{4}$

______ ______

 ISBN: 9780170447379

5 $\frac{4}{9}$ $\frac{3}{7}$

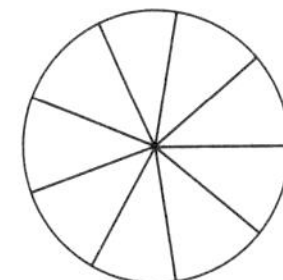

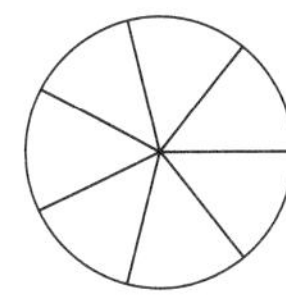

6 $\frac{3}{8}$ $\frac{4}{10}$

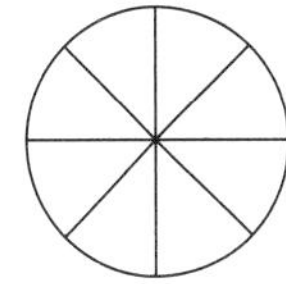

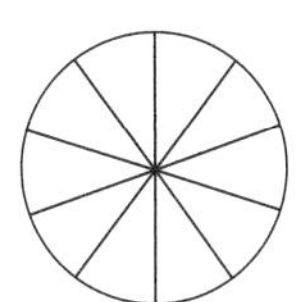

7 **a** Shade each diagram to match the fraction.

$\frac{2}{3}$ 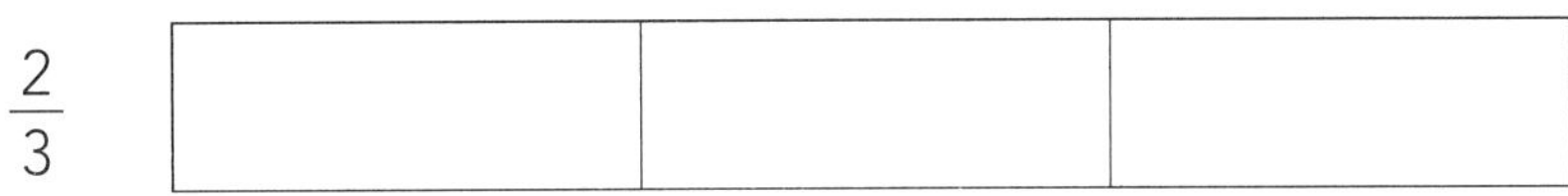

$\frac{5}{8}$ 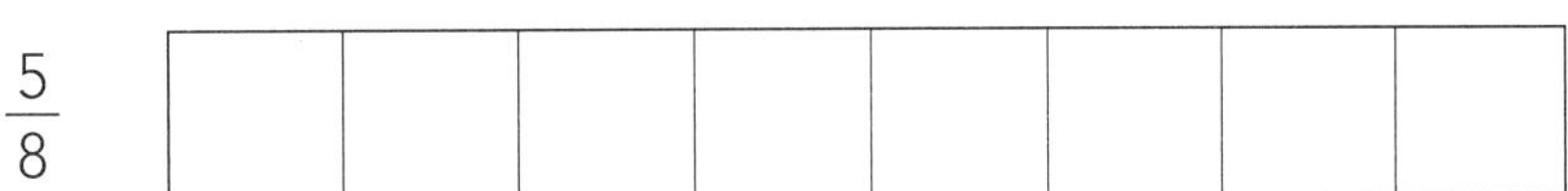

$\frac{3}{4}$ 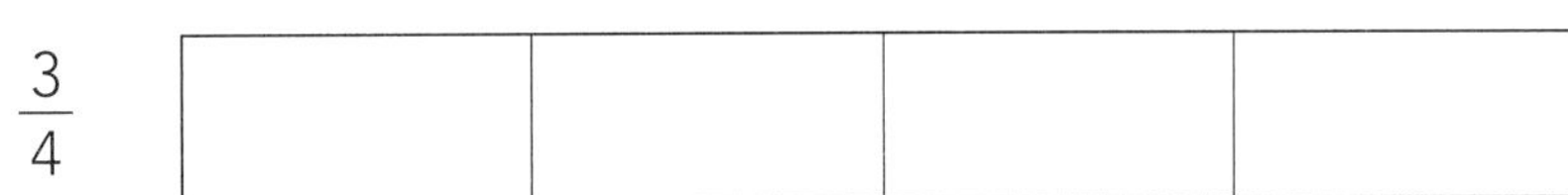

b Put these three fractions in order.

Largest ________ ________ ________ Smallest

8 **a** Shade each diagram to match the fraction.

$\frac{2}{6}$ 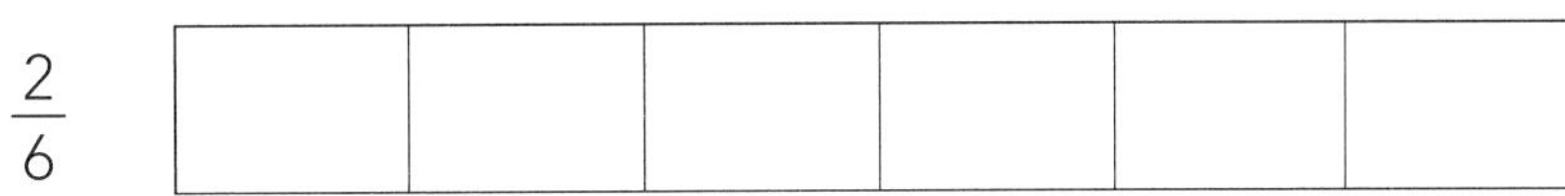

$\frac{3}{12}$ 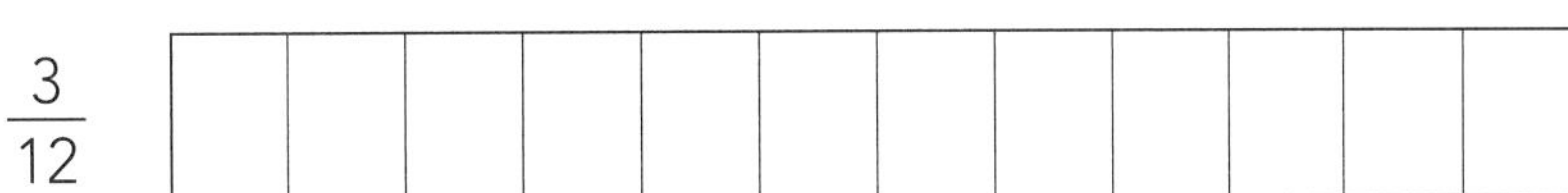

$\frac{4}{9}$ 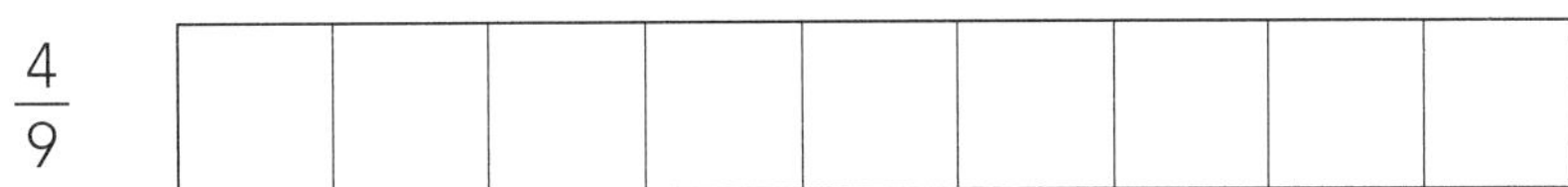

b Put these three fractions in order.

Largest ________ ________ ________ Smallest

ISBN: 9780170447379

9 Use Method 1 and Method 2 to determine which fraction is larger.

	Method 1	**Method 2**
	Shade the diagrams to match the questions.	Find the lowest common multiple of the denominator.
a	Which is larger, $\frac{1}{3}$ or $\frac{2}{5}$? $\frac{1}{3}$ [| |] $\frac{2}{5}$ [| | | |] The larger fraction is ______.	The LCM of 3 and 5 is **15**. x 5 $\frac{1}{3} = \frac{\quad}{15}$ x 5 x 3 $\frac{2}{5} = \frac{\quad}{15}$ x 3
b	Which is larger, $\frac{4}{7}$ or $\frac{3}{5}$? $\frac{4}{7}$ [| | | | | |] $\frac{3}{5}$ [| | | |] The larger fraction is ______.	The LCM of 7 and 5 is **35**. x ____ $\frac{4}{7} = \frac{\quad}{35}$ x 5 x ____ $\frac{3}{5} = \frac{\quad}{35}$ x 7
c	Which is larger, $\frac{3}{10}$ or $\frac{1}{3}$? $\frac{3}{10}$ [| | | | | | | | |] $\frac{1}{3}$ [| |] The larger fraction is ______.	The LCM of $\frac{3}{10}$ and $\frac{1}{3}$ is **30**. x ____ $\frac{3}{10} = \frac{\quad}{30}$ x ____ x ____ $\frac{1}{3} = \frac{\quad}{30}$ x ____

  ISBN: 9780170447379

	Method 1	Method 2
d	Which is larger, $\frac{3}{5}$ or $\frac{2}{3}$? $\frac{3}{5}$ $\frac{2}{3}$ The larger fraction is ______________.	The LCM of 5 and 3 is **15**. $\frac{3}{5} = \frac{\quad}{\mathbf{15}}$ (x ____ , x ____) $\frac{2}{3} = \frac{\quad}{\mathbf{15}}$ (x ____ , x ____)
e	Which is larger, $\frac{3}{8}$ or $\frac{1}{3}$? $\frac{3}{8}$ $\frac{1}{3}$ The larger fraction is ______________.	The LCM of 8 and 3 is ______. $\frac{3}{8} = \frac{\quad}{\quad}$ (x ____ , x ____) $\frac{1}{3} = \frac{\quad}{\quad}$ (x ____ , x ____)
f	Which is larger, $\frac{4}{5}$ or $\frac{5}{6}$? $\frac{4}{5}$ $\frac{5}{6}$ The larger fraction is ______________.	The LCM of 5 and 6 is ______. $\frac{4}{5} = \frac{\quad}{\quad}$ (x ____ , x ____) $\frac{5}{6} = \frac{\quad}{\quad}$ (x ____ , x ____)

Converting between improper and mixed fractions

- An **improper** fraction is when the numerator is bigger than the denominator.

Example: $\frac{3}{2}$

- A **mixed** fraction is a combination of a whole number and a fraction.

Example: $1\frac{1}{2}$

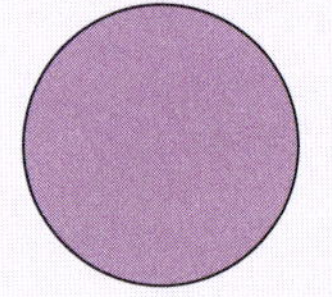
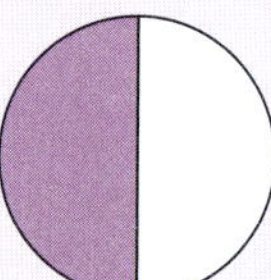

Complete the table. The first one has been done for you.

	Improper fraction	Mixed fraction
1	$\frac{5}{4}$ Five quarters	$1\frac{1}{4}$ One and one quarter
2	___ ________________	___ ________________
3	___ ________________	___ ________________
4	___ ________________	___ ________________

ISBN: 9780170447379

Converting improper fractions to mixed fractions

Example: Convert $\frac{13}{5}$ into a mixed fraction.

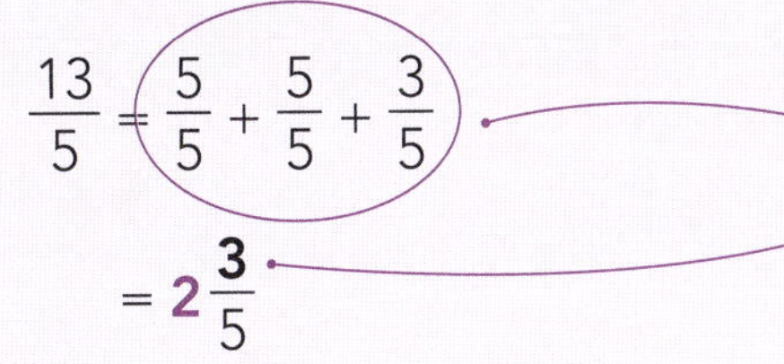

$\frac{13}{5} = \frac{5}{5} + \frac{5}{5} + \frac{3}{5}$

There are **2** lots of 5 in 13, with **3** fifths left over.

$= 2\frac{3}{5}$

Complete the following.

5 $\frac{19}{7} = \frac{7}{7} + \frac{7}{7} + \frac{5}{7} = 2\frac{\square}{7}$

6 $\frac{15}{4} = \frac{4}{4} + \frac{4}{4} + \frac{4}{4} + \frac{3}{4} = 3\frac{\square}{4}$

7 $\frac{19}{6} = \frac{6}{6} + \frac{6}{6} + \frac{6}{6} + \frac{\square}{6} = 3\frac{\square}{6}$

8 $\frac{11}{3} = \frac{3}{3} + \frac{3}{3} + \frac{3}{3} + \frac{\square}{3} = 3\frac{\square}{3}$

9 $\frac{7}{2} = \frac{\square}{2} + \frac{\square}{2} + \frac{\square}{2} + \frac{\square}{2} =$

10 $\frac{12}{5} =$

Converting mixed fractions to improper fractions

Example: Convert $2\frac{1}{5}$ into an improper fraction.

$2\frac{1}{5} = \frac{5}{5} + \frac{5}{5} + \frac{1}{5}$

There are **2** lots of **5** fifths (**10** fifths), with **1** fifth left over.

$= \frac{11}{5}$

Complete the following.

11 $2\frac{3}{4} = \frac{4}{4} + \frac{4}{4} + \frac{3}{4} = \frac{\square}{4}$

12 $3\frac{2}{5} = \frac{5}{5} + \frac{5}{5} + \frac{5}{5} + \frac{2}{5} = \frac{\square}{5}$

13 $1\frac{5}{7} = \frac{\square}{7} + \frac{\square}{7} = \frac{\square}{7}$

14 $3\frac{1}{3} = \frac{\square}{3} + \frac{\square}{3} + \frac{\square}{3} + \frac{\square}{3} = \frac{\square}{3}$

15 $4\frac{1}{2} =$ $= \frac{\square}{2}$

16 $3\frac{1}{6} =$

Adding and subtracting fractions

With the same denominators

- To add or subtract fractions with the **same denominator**, you add or subtract the numerator. The denominator does not change.

Example: $\frac{1}{4} + \frac{1}{4} = \frac{2}{4}$

1 + 1 is 2.

The denominator remains a 4.

Complete the shading and fill in the missing numbers to add and subtract fractions.

1 $\frac{1}{\ } + \frac{1}{\ } = \frac{\ }{\ }$

2 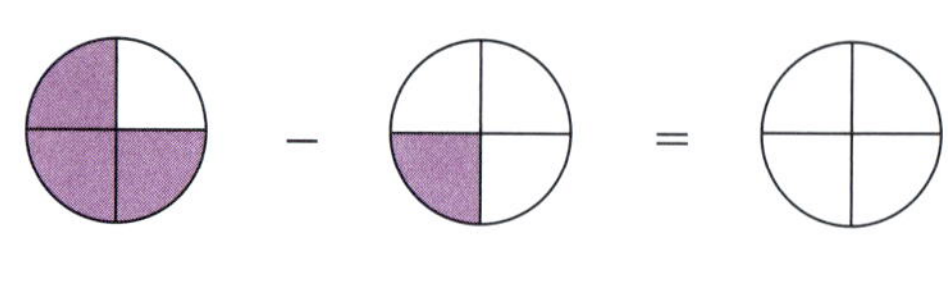

$\frac{\ }{5} + \frac{\ }{5} = \frac{\ }{5}$

3 $\frac{1}{\ } + \frac{2}{\ } = \frac{\ }{4}$

4 $\frac{3}{\ } - \frac{1}{\ } = \frac{\ }{4}$

5 $\frac{\ }{6} - \frac{\ }{6} = \frac{\ }{\ }$

6 

$\frac{\ }{\ } + \frac{\ }{\ } = \frac{\ }{\ }$

7 $\frac{3}{5} + \frac{1}{5} =$

8 $\frac{5}{8} - \frac{3}{8} =$

9 $\frac{2}{6} + \frac{1}{6} =$

10 $\frac{2}{4} - \frac{1}{4} =$

 ISBN: 9780170447379

With different denominators

- If the denominators are different, then it can be useful to use pictures to solve the calculation.

Examples:

1 $\frac{1}{4} + \frac{1}{2} = \frac{3}{4}$

+ = 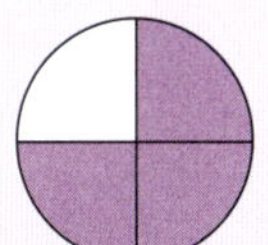

2 $\frac{1}{2} - \frac{1}{3} = \frac{1}{6}$

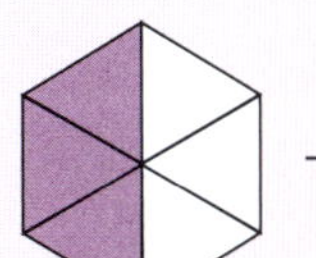 − 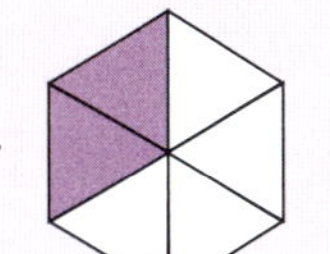 = 

Join the dots to match each calculation with its correct picture.

11

$\frac{1}{3} + \frac{1}{6} = \frac{3}{6}$ • • − 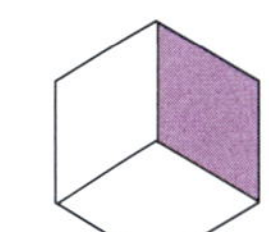 =

$\frac{9}{12} - \frac{1}{4} = \frac{6}{12}$ • • 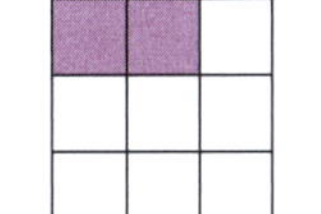 + 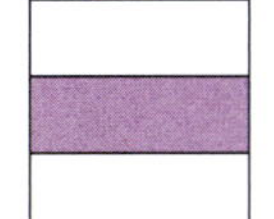 =

$\frac{5}{6} - \frac{1}{3} = \frac{3}{6}$ • • 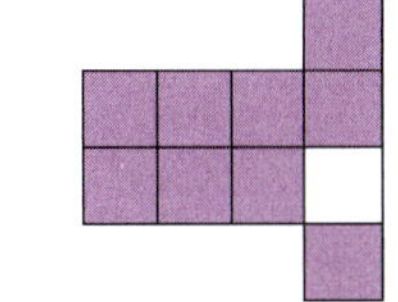 − 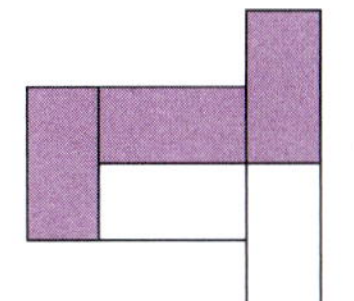 = 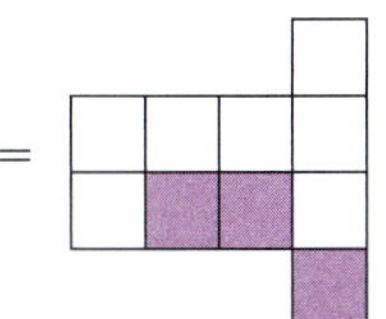

$\frac{2}{9} + \frac{1}{3} = \frac{5}{9}$ • •  + 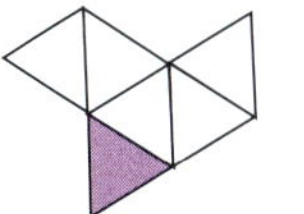 = 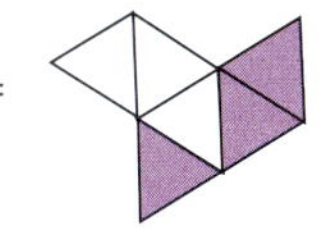

$\frac{5}{8} + \frac{1}{4} = \frac{7}{8}$ • • 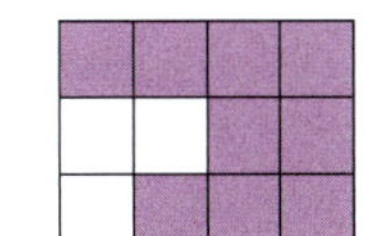 − 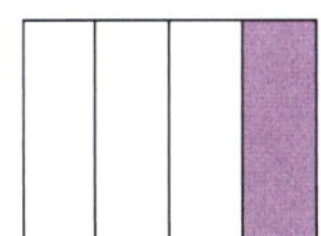 = 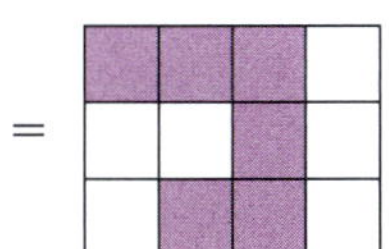

$\frac{9}{10} - \frac{3}{5} = \frac{3}{10}$ • • + =

ISBN: 9780170447379

Complete the shading and missing values for these calculations.

12

$\frac{\ }{6} + \frac{1}{\ } = \frac{5}{\ }$

13

$\frac{3}{\ } - \frac{\ }{2} = \frac{\ }{4}$

14

$\frac{\ }{6} + \frac{2}{\ } = \frac{\ }{6}$

15

$\frac{8}{\ } - \frac{1}{\ } = \frac{\ }{\ }$

16

$\frac{1}{\ } + \frac{\ }{8} = \frac{\ }{\ }$

17

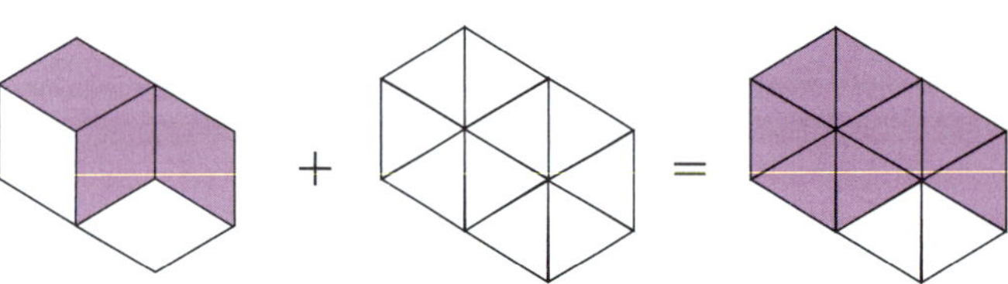

$\frac{3}{\ } + \frac{2}{10} = \frac{\ }{10}$ or $\frac{\ }{5}$

18

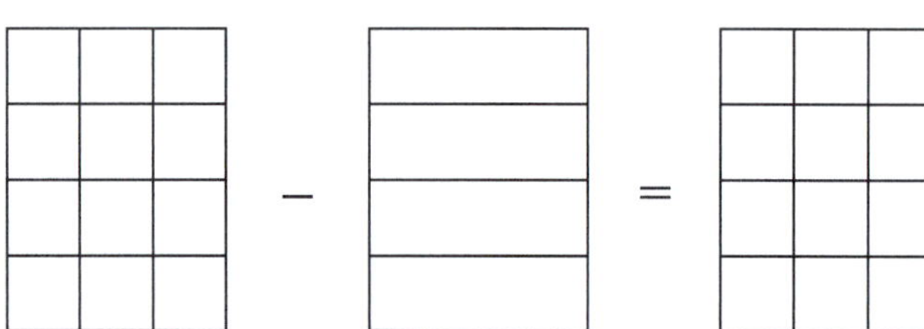

$\frac{\ }{\ } - \frac{3}{4} = 0$

 ISBN: 9780170447379

Multiplying fractions

- To multiply fractions, **multiply the numerators** and then **multiply the denominators**.
- Mixed fractions must be converted to improper fractions first.
- If possible, simplify the answer and write it as a mixed fraction.

Examples:

1 $\frac{2}{3} \times \frac{1}{2} = \frac{2 \times 1}{3 \times 2}$

$= \frac{2}{6}$

$= \frac{1}{3}$

2 $\frac{2}{3} \times \frac{3}{5} = \frac{2 \times 3}{3 \times 5}$

$= \frac{6}{15}$

$= \frac{2}{5}$

Simplify.

Multiply these fractions and simplify when possible.

1 $\frac{1}{4} \times \frac{1}{3} =$ ______
= ______
= ______

2 $\frac{2}{5} \times \frac{1}{2} =$ ______
= ______
= ______

3 $\frac{3}{4} \times \frac{1}{5} =$ ______
= ______
= ______

4 $\frac{3}{5} \times \frac{1}{2} =$ ______
= ______
= ______

5 $\frac{3}{4} \times \frac{2}{5} =$ ______
= ______
= ______

6 $\frac{3}{8} \times \frac{1}{6} =$ ______
= ______
= ______

7 $\frac{1}{5} \times \frac{4}{7} =$ ______
= ______
= ______

8 $\frac{2}{3} \times \frac{3}{6} =$ ______
= ______
= ______

9 $\frac{3}{2} \times \frac{1}{4} =$ ______
= ______
= ______

10 $1\frac{1}{4} \times \frac{2}{3} =$ ______
= ______
= ______

ISBN: 9780170447379

Dividing fractions

Reciprocals

The **reciprocal** of the fraction $\frac{a}{b}$ is $\frac{b}{a}$.

- You may like to think of this as 'turning the fraction upside down'.
- To find the reciprocal of a mixed fraction, you must convert it to an improper fraction first.

Examples: **1** The reciprocal of $\frac{7}{9}$ is $\frac{9}{7}$.

2 $7\frac{3}{4} = \frac{31}{4}$, so the reciprocal of $7\frac{3}{4}$ is $\frac{4}{31}$.

3 $5 = \frac{5}{1}$, so the reciprocal of 5 is $\frac{1}{5}$.

Write reciprocals of the following numbers.

1 $\frac{2}{3}$ Reciprocal = ____________

2 $\frac{1}{4}$ Reciprocal = ____________

3 $\frac{5}{4}$ Reciprocal = ____________

4 $\frac{5}{6}$ Reciprocal = ____________

5 $\frac{7}{8}$ Reciprocal = ____________

6 $\frac{8}{6}$ Reciprocal = ____________

7 $\frac{4}{7}$ Reciprocal = ____________

8 3 Reciprocal = ____________

9 $1\frac{1}{3}$ Reciprocal = ____________

10 $1\frac{3}{4}$ Reciprocal = ____________

To divide fractions

- Mixed fractions must be converted to improper fractions first.
- Trick to dividing fractions:
  1 Leave the first fraction unchanged.
  2 Write the reciprocal of the second fraction. (Turn it upside down.)
  3 Multiply the two together.

If possible, simplify the answer and write it as a mixed fraction.

Example:

$$\frac{3}{4} \div \frac{1}{3} = \frac{3}{4} \times \frac{3}{1}$$

Multiply by the reciprocal of the second fraction.

$$= \frac{3 \times 3}{4 \times 1}$$

Multiply instead of divide.

$$= \frac{9}{4}$$

Change to a mixed fraction.

$$= 2\frac{1}{4}$$

 ISBN: 9780170447379

Divide these fractions and simplify when possible. Where appropriate, write your answers as mixed fractions.

11 $\frac{1}{2} \div \frac{2}{3} =$ __________
= __________
= __________

12 $\frac{1}{3} \div \frac{1}{5} =$ __________
= __________
= __________

13 $\frac{3}{4} \div \frac{1}{6} =$ __________
= __________
= __________

14 $\frac{1}{3} \div \frac{4}{5} =$ __________
= __________
= __________

15 $\frac{2}{5} \div \frac{1}{6} =$ __________
= __________
= __________

16 $\frac{3}{7} \div \frac{1}{2} =$ __________
= __________
= __________

17 $\frac{3}{4} \div \frac{1}{4} =$ __________
= __________
= __________

18 $\frac{5}{6} \div \frac{3}{2} =$ __________
= __________
= __________

19 $\frac{4}{7} \div \frac{4}{5} =$ __________
= __________
= __________

20 $\frac{1}{5} \div 5 =$ __________
= __________
= __________

21 $3 \div \frac{1}{2} =$ __________
= __________
= __________

22 $\frac{1}{3} \div 1\frac{1}{4} =$ __________
= __________
= __________

ISBN: 9780170447379

Fractions of a quantity

Remember that '**of**' means you must '**multiply**'.

Example: $\frac{1}{4}$ **of** 12 = $\frac{1}{4}$ **x** 12

= $\frac{1}{4} \times \frac{12}{1}$

= $\frac{12}{4}$

= 3

Replace the word '**of**' with a **x** sign.

Remember that '12' means 12 wholes, or $\frac{12}{1}$.

Answer the following questions.

1 $\frac{1}{3}$ of 18 = ______
= ______
= ______

2 $\frac{1}{2}$ of 42 = ______
= ______
= ______

3 $\frac{1}{5}$ of 25 = ______
= ______
= ______

4 $\frac{1}{6}$ of 42 = ______
= ______
= ______

5 $\frac{2}{3}$ of 90 = ______
= ______
= ______

6 $\frac{3}{4}$ of 24 = ______
= ______
= ______

7 $\frac{3}{5}$ of 30 = ______
= ______
= ______

8 $\frac{3}{2}$ of 16 = ______
= ______
= ______

9 $1\frac{1}{3}$ of 15 = ______
= ______
= ______

10 $1\frac{1}{4}$ of 24 = ______
= ______
= ______

ISBN: 9780170447379

Mixing it up

1 Simplify this fraction:

$$\frac{18}{30} = \_\_$$

2 What is the reciprocal of $\frac{4}{1}$?

$\_\_$

3 Convert this to a mixed fraction:

$$\frac{16}{5} =$$

4 Calculate: $\frac{3}{4}$ of 28

= ____________________

5 Calculate these.

a $\frac{1}{5} \times \frac{3}{4} =$

b $\frac{1}{5} \div \frac{3}{4} =$

c $\frac{4}{5} + \frac{1}{2} =$

d $\frac{7}{8} - \frac{1}{6} =$

6 Convert this into an improper fraction:

$$2\frac{5}{7} =$$

7 Find an equivalent fraction to:

$$\frac{2}{7} = \_\_$$

8

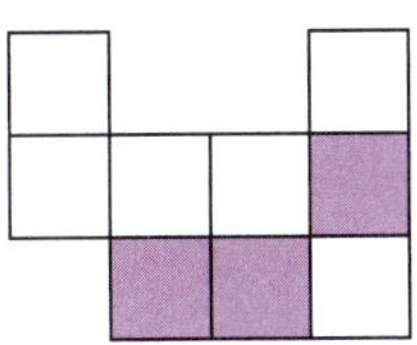

Shaded ______

Not shaded ______

9 Calculate:

$\frac{1}{5} \times 1\frac{1}{2} =$ ____________________

10 Fill in the values to make all the fractions equivalent.

$$\frac{1}{4} = \frac{\_\_}{12} = \frac{4}{\_\_} = \frac{\_\_}{20} = \frac{\_\_}{24} = \frac{7}{\_\_} = \frac{\_\_}{48}$$

ISBN: 9780170447379

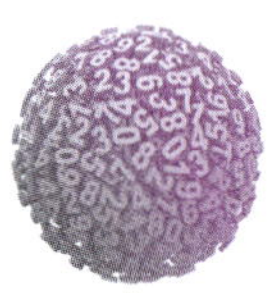

Challenge 2

1 Gillian and Greg ordered a pizza each. Gillian managed to eat $\frac{2}{3}$ of hers, Greg ate $\frac{16}{25}$ of his. Who ate more pizza?

2 Fran's class sat a Science test, and it is announced that $\frac{3}{4}$ of the class has passed. If the class has 32 students, how many passed the Science test?

3 $\frac{1}{5}$ of the lollies in a bag are green, $\frac{2}{3}$ are red. If Wiremu ate all the green and red lollies, what fraction of the packet is left?

4 Duncan bought 12 marbles on Wednesday and another 36 on Thursday. On Friday he gave $\frac{1}{6}$ of these marbles to his friend Sam. How many marbles does he have left?

5 Use each number from the list once only in order to complete the calculations below.

1	1	1	2	2	3	3	3	4	5	5	6	9	9	10	12	12

$\frac{4}{8} = \frac{\ }{2}$	$\frac{1}{\ } = \frac{\ }{\ }$	$\frac{3}{\ } = \frac{\ }{3}$
$\frac{2}{8} = \frac{1}{\ }$	$\frac{\ }{10} = \frac{\ }{2}$	$\frac{\ }{4} = \frac{9}{\ }$
$\frac{\ }{6} = \frac{1}{\ }$	$\frac{1}{4} = \frac{\ }{\ }$	$\frac{2}{3} = \frac{\ }{\ }$

 ISBN: 9780170447379

Decimals

Place value

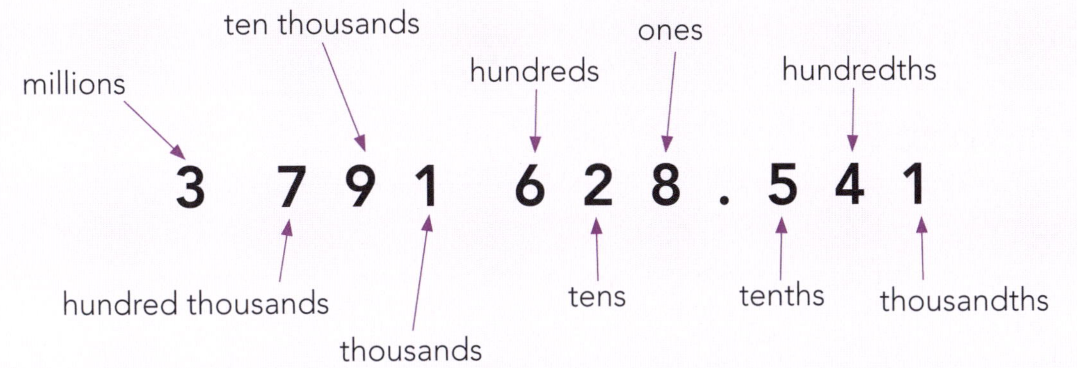

When converting numerals to words, split the number where the **gaps** occur.

Examples: 1 Write 15 263 748 in words.

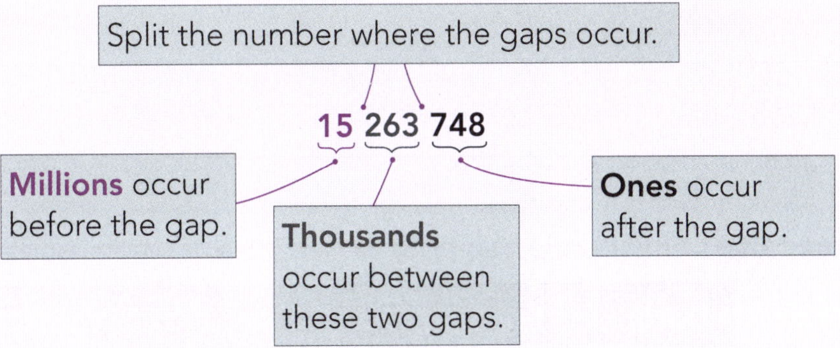

Fifteen million, **two hundred and sixty-three thousand**, **seven hundred and forty-eight** (ones).

2 Write 24 768.5 in words.

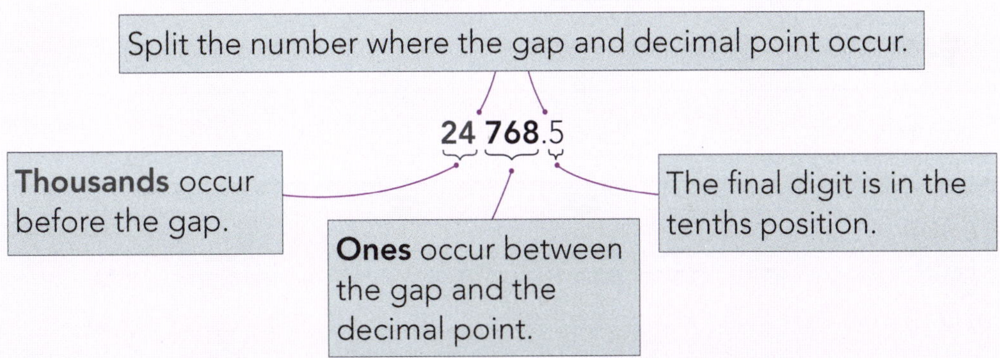

Twenty-four thousand, **seven hundred and sixty-eight** and five tenths.

Write down the value of the purple numerals as numbers and in words.

		Number	Words
1	12 **6**34	600	
2	2 3**5**4 176		Fifty thousand
3	5 3**4**1		
4	13**7** 789 100		
5	**8**10 240		
6	56**1** 266		
7	92 3**8**9		
8	**2**17 431 891		
9	7 **2**23		
10	6**9**1 864 265		

Write down the value of the purple numerals as decimals, fractions and in words.

		Decimal	Fraction	Words
11	0.**5**72		――	Five tenths
12	0.12**6**		$\frac{6}{1\,000}$	
13	23.6**4**1	0.04	――	
14	198.15**3**		――	
15	6.10**8**		――	
16	7.**2**13		――	
17	90.1**4**5		――	
18	0.02**9**		――	

 ISBN: 9780170447379

Write numbers using words.

19 1 253

____

20 52 674

____

21 801

____

22 25.7

____

23 246 197.8

____

24 301 642 121

____

25 0.12

____

26 300 192.9

____

27 100 001.43

____

Write numbers using numerals.

28 One hundred and ninety-two ______________

29 Thirty-four and nine tenths 34.9

30 Nine thousand, two hundred and seventeen ______________

31 One million, four hundred and fifty thousand and six ______________

32 Thirty-three thousandths ______________

33 Forty-five hundredths ______________

34 Eight hundred and thirty-two and four tenths ______________

35 Seven hundred thousand and forty-six ______________

36 Seventy-eight million, one hundred and fifty-three and nine tenths ______________

ISBN: 9780170447379

Decimals on number lines

Here is how to work out the size of each gap between ticks on a number line.

Step 1: Calculate the **distance** between two **labelled** points.
Distance = 0.9 – 0.2 = **0.7**.

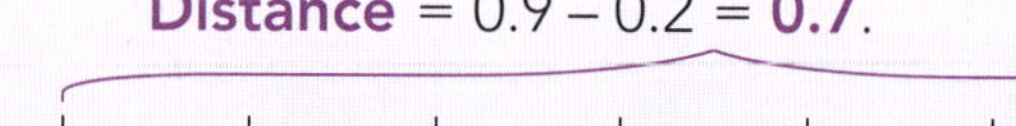

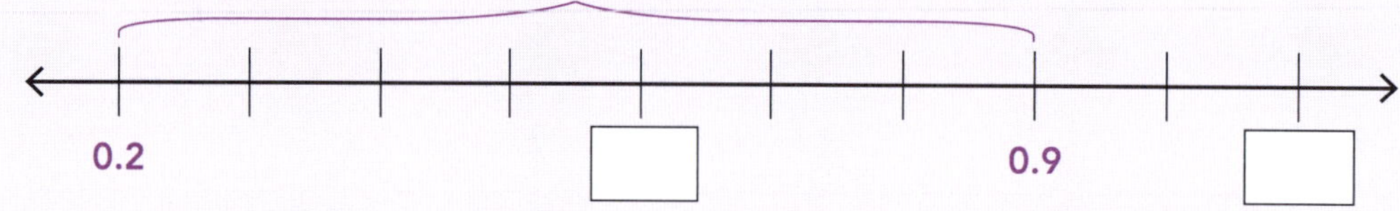

Step 2: Count the number of gaps between 0.2 and 0.9. **Number of gaps** = **7**.

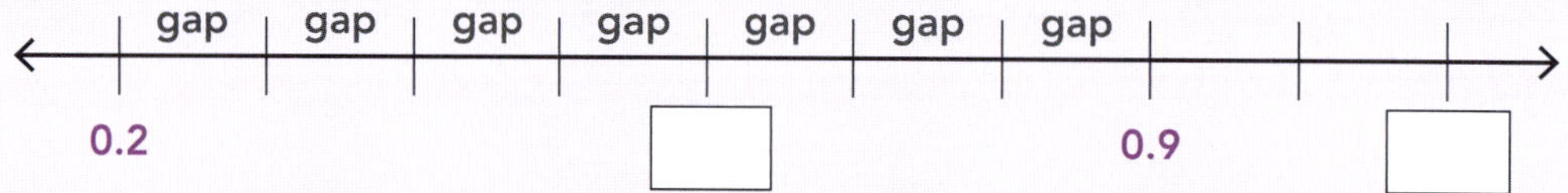

Step 3: Divide the distance by the number of gaps: $\frac{0.7}{7} = 0.1$.

Step 4: Add 0.1 after each gap along the number line.

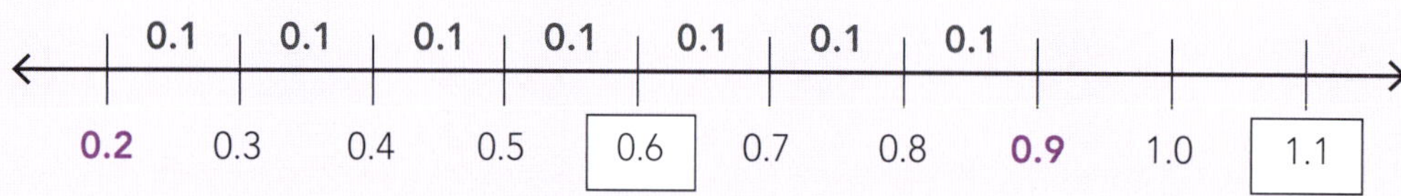

Calculate the size of each gap and write the missing decimals on the number lines.

1

2.4 ☐ 2.8 ☐

Size of gap = $\frac{\textbf{interval}}{\textbf{gaps}}$ =

$\frac{\textbf{2.8 – 2.4}}{\textbf{4}} = \frac{\textbf{0.4}}{\textbf{4}} =$

2

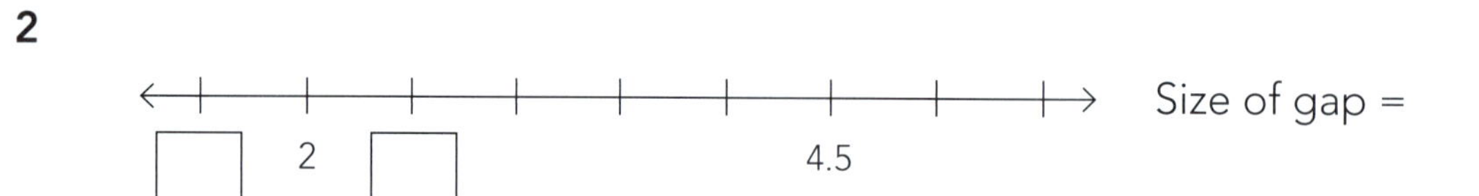

Size of gap =

3

Size of gap =

4

Size of gap =

 ISBN: 9780170447379

5 Write decimal values for each point along the number line. Choose the most appropriate values from the list below. You will not need all the points on the list.

0.2	0.05	2.1	0.8
0.6	0.3	1.2	0.7
0.1	1.1	0.9	0.5

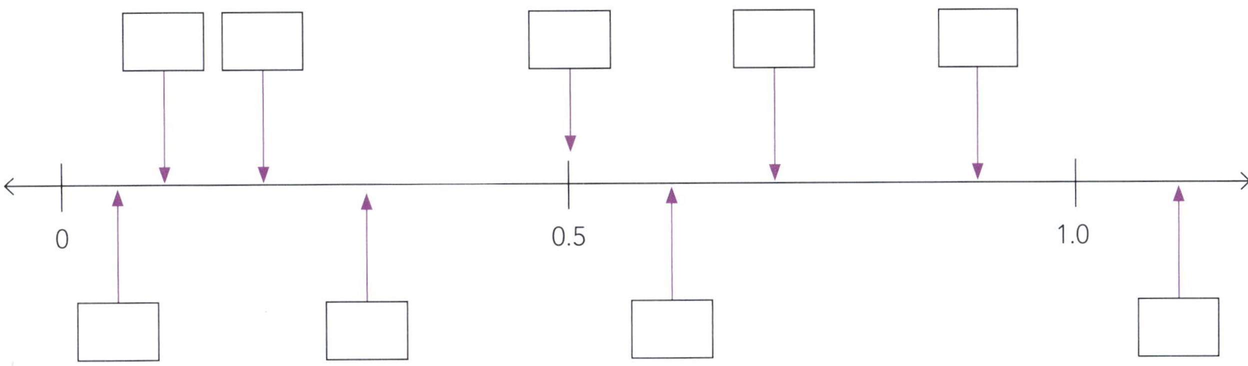

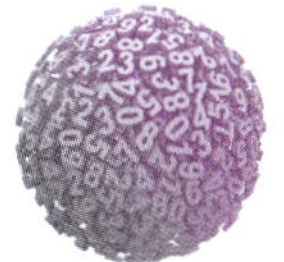

Challenge 3

1 Write decimal values for each point along the number line. Choose the most appropriate values from the list below. You will not need all the points on the list.

19.5	1.9	21.7	13.8	11.4	15.0
10.3	0.6	3.4	9.5	14.3	16.6
5.8	4.9	2.1	6.9	18.1	8.2

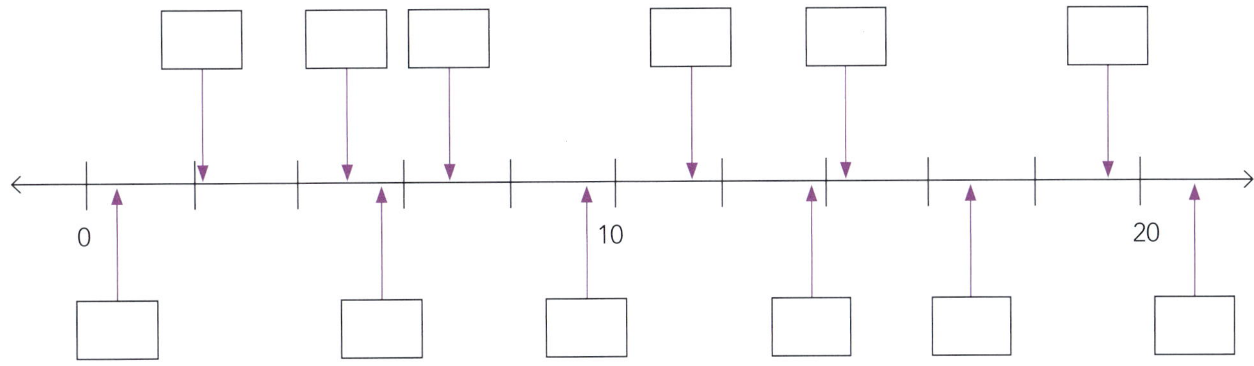

ISBN: 9780170447379

2 Fill in the white squares to complete this cross-number. You will need to use a decimal point (•) in some squares.

1	2		3	4	5			6
			7				8	
9		10				11		
12	13				14		15	
16						17		
18			19		20			
		21		22				
23			24				25	
		26						

ACROSS

1 Two million, one hundred and thirty-four thousand, two hundred and ninety-seven.
7 The value of the 6 in 3679.
8 Forty-four.
10 Eight hundred and seventeen and nine tenths.
12 Ninety-two hundred and five.
14 Four thousand, three hundred and eleven.
16 The value of the 4 in 487.2.
17 Five and seven tenths.
18 Four thousand and eight.
20 One thousand, five hundred and ninety.
21 Nineteen thousand, six hundred.
23 The value of the 9 in 6 793.
24 Nine and four tenths.
26 Eight million, nine hundred thousand, four hundred and sixteen.

DOWN

2 The value of the 1 in 812.
3 Four thousand, six hundred and fifteen.
4 Two hundred and seven.
5 Ninety and four tenths.
6 One million, four hundred and sixty-one thousand, seven hundred.
9 Nine million, nine hundred and forty-four thousand, nine hundred and ninety-four.
10 Eighty thousand and one.
11 Ninety-three thousand, five hundred and fifty.
13 The value of the 2 in 63 450 219.
15 One and nine tenths.
19 Eight thousand, nine hundred and ninety-nine.
20 One thousand and forty.
22 Six and zero tenths.
25 Seventy-one.

ISBN: 9780170447379

Comparing decimals

- To determine which decimal is larger, you need to consider the place values of each digit, starting from the left.

Examples:

1 Identify the larger number: **52.8** or **52.9**.

Step 1: Arrange the numbers with the **decimal points lined up** vertically:

52.8
52.9

The decimal points **must** be in line.

Step 2: Start at the left, and look for the **first pair of digits that is different**:

52 | **.8**
52 | **.9**

The first **two** digits are the same.

Step 3: Decide which is larger, **8** or **9**. 9 is larger, so 52.9 is the larger number.

2 Identify the larger number: **24.15** or **24.12**.

Step 1: Arrange the numbers with the decimal points lined up vertically:

24.15
24.12

Step 2: Start at the left, and look for the **first pair of digits that is different**:

24.1 | **5**
24.1 | **2**

The first **three** digits are the same.

Step 3: Decide which is larger, **5** or **2**. 5 is larger, so 24.15 is the larger number.

Highlight the larger number.

1	13.5	13.4	**2**	1 457	1 458
3	9.52	9.51	**4**	56.46	56.47
5	423.8	423.9	**6**	8.41	8.40
7	101.0	110.0	**8**	6.01	6.10
9	0.94	0.95	**10**	0.67	0.76
11	0.8	0.80	**12**	8.47	8.74

Write down the following decimals.

13 8.1 increased by one tenth. ______

14 14.6 increased by three tens. ______

15 36.5 increased by four ones. ______

16 60.04 increased by eight tenths. ______

17 1463 increased by five thousand. ______

18 234.1 increased by two hundred. ______

19 0.36 increased by two hundredths. ______

20 70.2 increased by sixteen ones. ______

Rearrange the following sets of digits in order to make the smallest and largest numbers possible. You must use all the digits (zero can't be the first digit).

		Smallest	**Largest**
21	7 1 2 5	______	______
22	8 9 2 0 6	______	______
23	1 4 2 6 9 8	______	______
24	3 1 0	______	______
25	0 9 3 1 2 1 4	______	______

Place these decimals in ascending order (smallest to largest).

26 5.61 5.16 6.51 6.15 ______ ______ ______ ______

27 0.11 0.01 0.00 0.10 ______ ______ ______ ______

28 4.14 4.11 4.44 4.41 ______ ______ ______ ______

29 0.98 0.99 0.89 0.88 ______ ______ ______ ______

30 0.02 0.20 2.00 2.02 ______ ______ ______ ______

 ISBN: 9780170447379

Using decimals to compare fractions

You can compare fractions by:
1 converting the fractions to decimals using your calculator,
2 then comparing by identifying which number is larger.

Examples: Identify which fraction is larger out of the two.

1 $\frac{9}{25}$ or $\frac{7}{20}$

$\frac{9}{25} = 0.3|$**6**

$\frac{7}{20} = 0.3|$**5**

Use a button that looks like S⇔D or a b/c or F↔D.

6 is larger than **5**, so $\frac{9}{25}$ is larger than $\frac{7}{20}$.

2 $\frac{13}{20}$ or $\frac{10}{16}$

$\frac{13}{20} = 0.6|$**5**

$\frac{10}{16} = 0.6|$**2**5

When one decimal has more digits, compare only the digits next to the line. **5** is larger than **2**.

5 is larger than **2**, so $\frac{13}{20}$ is larger than $\frac{10}{16}$.

Convert the following fractions to decimals using your calculator, and conclude which is larger and which is smaller.

1

$\frac{3}{5}$ = __________

$\frac{14}{20}$ = __________

______ is larger than ______

2

$\frac{11}{25}$ = __________

$\frac{9}{20}$ = __________

______ is larger than ______

3

$\frac{3}{4}$ = __________

$\frac{37}{50}$ = __________

______ is larger than ______

4

$\frac{13}{25}$ = __________

$\frac{27}{50}$ = __________

______ is larger than ______

5

$\frac{11}{100}$ = __________

$\frac{8}{80}$ = __________

______ is larger than ______

6

$\frac{21}{64}$ = __________

$\frac{5}{16}$ = __________

______ is larger than ______

ISBN: 9780170447379

7

$\frac{22}{25}$ = ______________ ________ is larger

$\frac{7}{8}$ = ______________ than ________

8

$\frac{3}{8}$ = ______________ ________ is larger

$\frac{19}{50}$ = ______________ than ________

9

$\frac{7}{16}$ = ______________ ________ is larger

$\frac{219}{500}$ = ______________ than ________

10

$\frac{22}{64}$ = ______________ ________ is larger

$\frac{4297}{12500}$ = ______________ than ________

11

$\frac{1}{4}$ = ______________ ________ is larger

$\frac{51}{200}$ = ______________ than ________

12

$\frac{23}{20}$ = ______________ ________ is larger

$\frac{6}{5}$ = ______________ than ________

13

$\frac{38}{25}$ = ______________ ________ is larger

$\frac{151}{100}$ = ______________ than ________

14

$\frac{1321}{500}$ = ______________ ________ is larger

$\frac{66}{25}$ = ______________ than ________

15 Complete this maze so that each fraction you move to is larger than the previous one. You may move horizontally or vertically but not diagonally.

Start

$\frac{1}{10}$	$\frac{2}{25}$	$\frac{13}{100}$	$\frac{4}{10}$	$\frac{6}{12}$	$\frac{17}{20}$	$\frac{32}{97}$
$\frac{1}{9}$	$\frac{3}{25}$	$\frac{7}{50}$	$\frac{1}{50}$	$\frac{12}{25}$	$\frac{13}{20}$	$\frac{4}{5}$
$\frac{3}{50}$	$\frac{4}{40}$	$\frac{3}{20}$	$\frac{26}{200}$	$\frac{29}{50}$	$\frac{3}{4}$	$\frac{41}{50}$
$\frac{33}{200}$	$\frac{41}{250}$	$\frac{81}{500}$	$\frac{4}{25}$	$\frac{11}{20}$	$\frac{27}{50}$	$\frac{17}{20}$
$\frac{1}{5}$	$\frac{4}{25}$	$\frac{161}{1000}$	$\frac{12}{25}$	$\frac{9}{18}$	$\frac{12}{25}$	$\frac{18}{20}$
$\frac{11}{50}$	$\frac{7}{20}$	$\frac{2}{5}$	$\frac{23}{50}$	$\frac{11}{25}$	$\frac{30}{50}$	**$\frac{99}{100}$**

Finish

 ISBN: 9780170447379

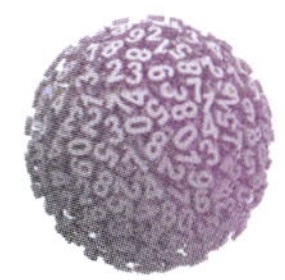

Percentages

- Percentages are a way of expressing a number **out of 100**.

Example:

26 out of 100 squares are purple.

$\frac{26}{100}$ is the same as 26%.

74 out of 100 squares are white.

$\frac{74}{100}$ is the same as 74%.

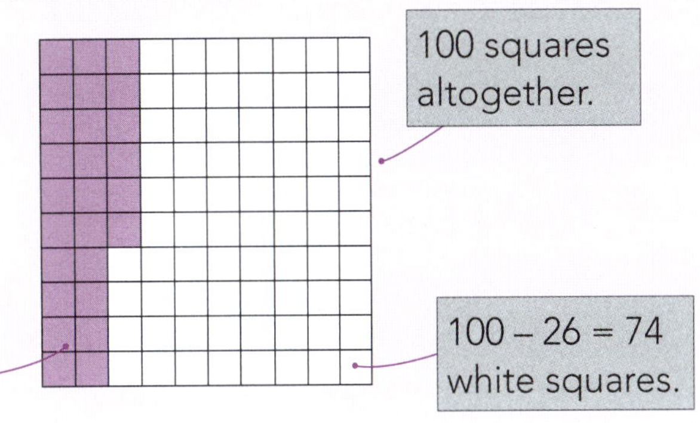

State the percentages shown in these diagrams.

1

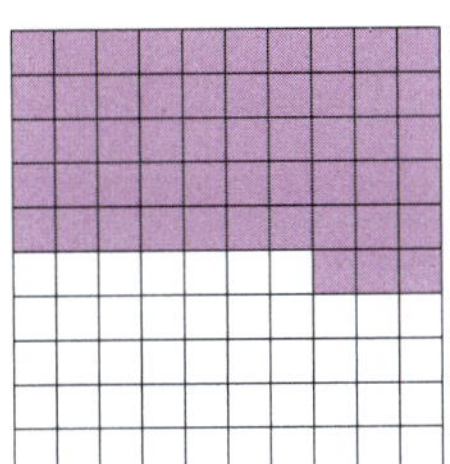

Percentage purple ______________

Percentage white ______________

2

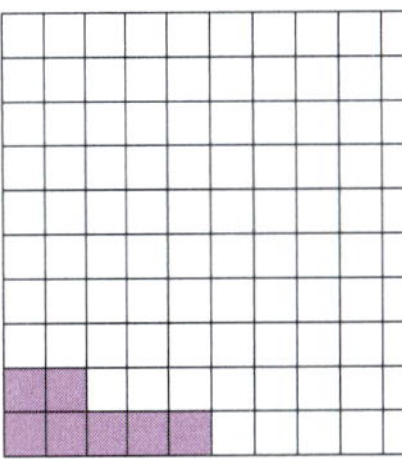

Percentage purple ______________

Percentage white ______________

3

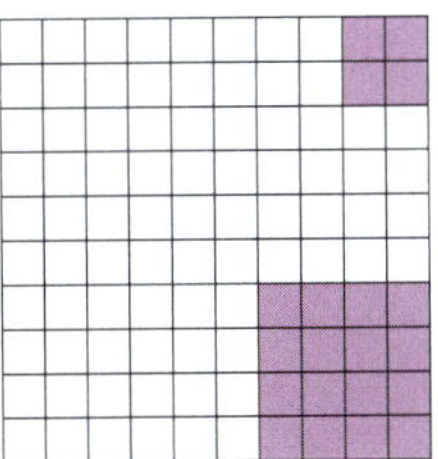

Percentage purple ______________

Percentage white ______________

4

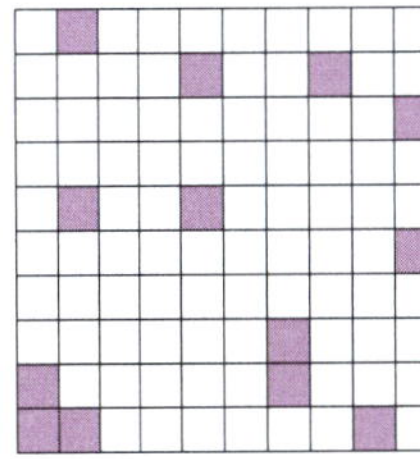

Percentage purple ______________

Percentage white ______________

5

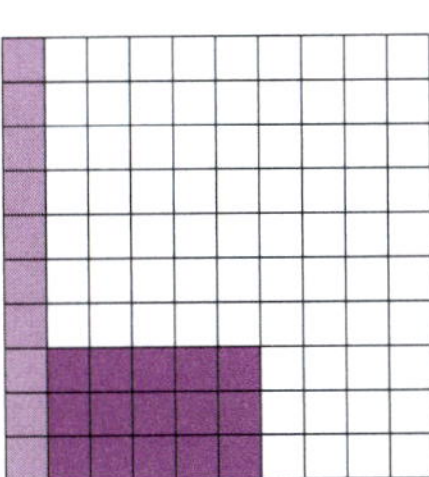

Percentage **dark purple** ______________

Percentage light purple ______________

Percentage white ______________

6

Percentage **dark purple** ______________

Percentage light purple ______________

Percentage white ______________

ISBN: 9780170447379

When there are not 100 squares

Example:

32 out of 50 squares are purple.

$\frac{32}{50}$ needs to be multiplied by 100 to make a percentage.

$\frac{32}{50}$ **x 100** = 64%, so 64% of the squares are purple.

$\frac{18}{50}$ of the squares are white.

$\frac{18}{50}$ **x 100** = 36%, so 36% of the squares are white.

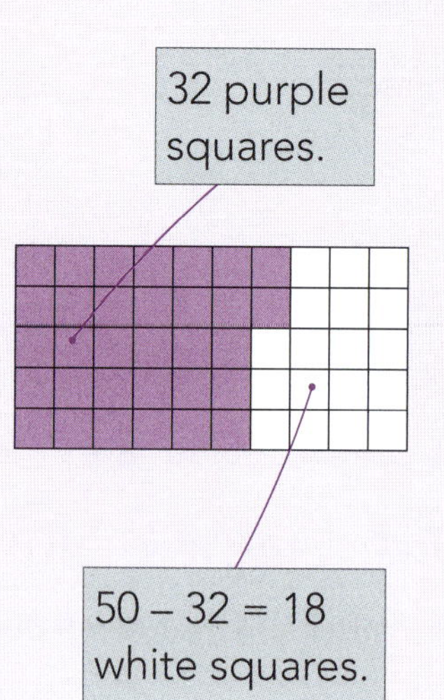

State the percentages shown in these diagrams.

7

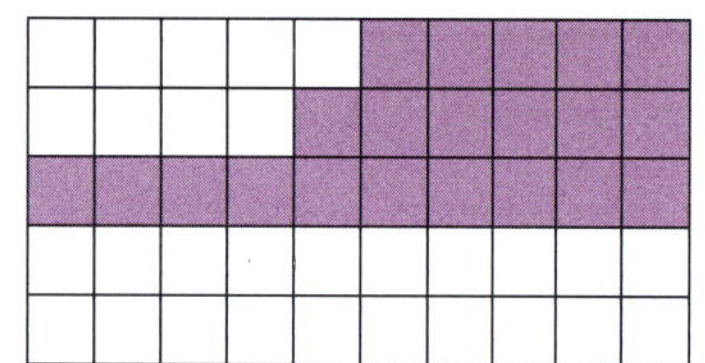

Percentage purple $\frac{\quad}{50}$ x **100** = ______

Percentage white $\frac{\quad}{50}$ x **100** = ______

8

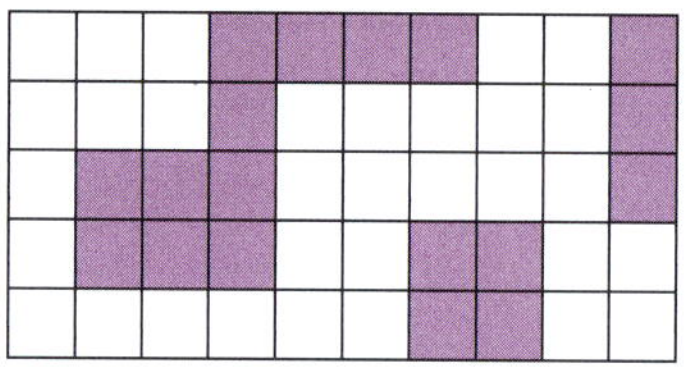

Percentage purple $\frac{\quad}{50}$ x **100** = ______

Percentage white $\frac{\quad}{50}$ x **100** = ______

9

Percentage purple $\frac{\quad}{30}$ x **100** = ______

Percentage white $\frac{\quad}{30}$ x **100** = ______

10

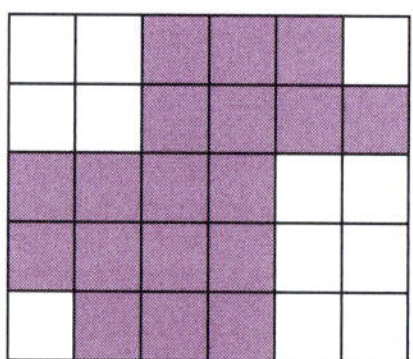

Percentage purple —— x **100** = ______

Percentage white —— x **100** = ______

11

Percentage purple —— x ______ = ______

Percentage white —— x ______ = ______

12

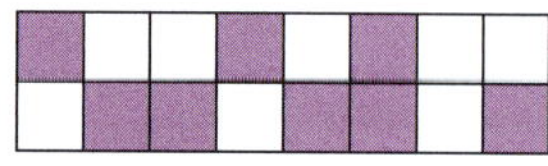

Percentage purple —— x ______ = ______

Percentage white —— x ______ = ______

 ISBN: 9780170447379

13 Join the dots between each diagram and its matching percentage.

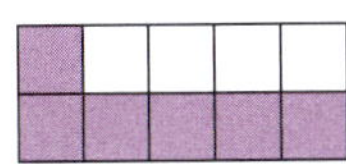	•	• 75%
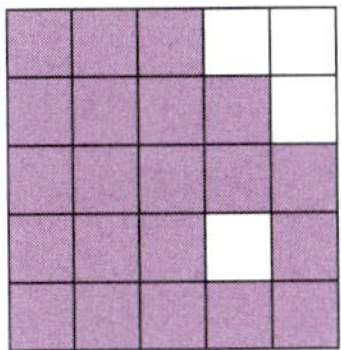	•	• 40%
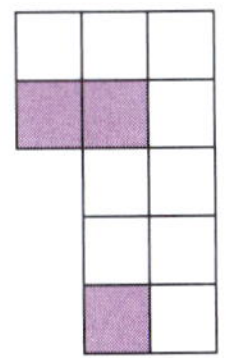	•	• 80%
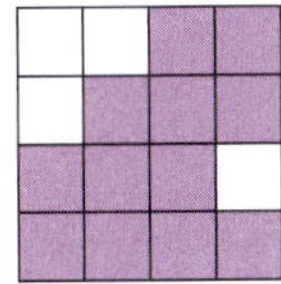	•	• 87.5%
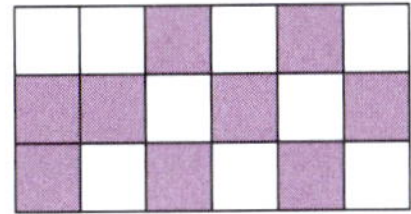	•	• 50%
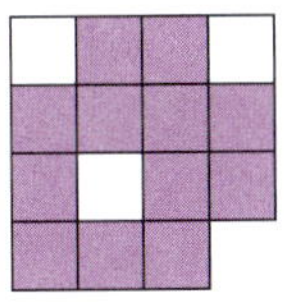	•	• 84%
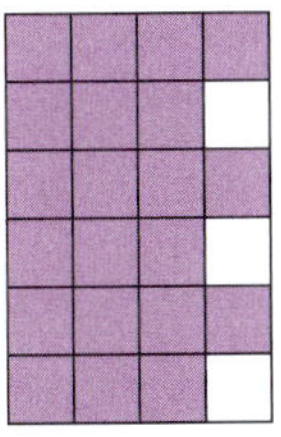	•	• 60%
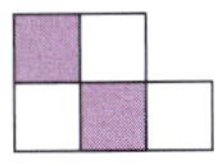	•	• 25%

ISBN: 9780170447379

Converting between fractions and percentages

Because percentages are out of 100,
- to change a fraction to a percentage, you **multiply by 100**
- to change a percentage to a fraction, you **divide by 100**.

Fractions to percentages: multiply by 100.

Examples: 1 $\frac{8}{25} = 32\%$ (× 100) 2 $\frac{36}{48} = 75\%$ (× 100)

On your calculator you can either multiply by 100 or use the % button.

Percentages to fractions: divide by 100 and then simplify the fraction.

Examples: 1 $44\% = \frac{44}{100} = \frac{11}{25}$ (÷ 100) 2 $74\% = \frac{74}{100} = \frac{37}{50}$ (÷ 100)

Convert these fractions into percentages.

1 $\frac{6}{20} =$ ____________ **2** $\frac{1}{5} =$ ____________

3 $\frac{3}{10} =$ ____________ **4** $\frac{3}{4} =$ ____________

5 $\frac{34}{40} =$ ____________ **6** $\frac{23}{25} =$ ____________

7 $\frac{3}{50} =$ ____________ **8** $\frac{19}{20} =$ ____________

9 $\frac{2}{5} =$ ____________ **10** $\frac{67}{100} =$ ____________

11 $\frac{7}{8} =$ ____________ **12** $\frac{17}{125} =$ ____________

13 $\frac{9}{5} =$ ____________ **14** $1\frac{1}{4} =$ ____________

 ISBN: 9780170447379

Convert these percentages into simplified fractions.

15 24% = ______________________ **16** 75% = ______________________

17 13% = ______________________ **18** 80% = ______________________

19 55% = ______________________ **20** 10% = ______________________

21 62% = ______________________ **22** 98% = ______________________

23 7% = ______________________ **24** 4% = ______________________

25 1% = ______________________ **26** 265% = ______________________

27 100% = ______________________ **28** 120% = ______________________

What's my number?

Circle the number that best fits all of the clues.

1 I am more than $\frac{2}{5}$.
I am not a percentage.
I am less than 80%.
Written as a fraction, my numerator is 9.

$\frac{37}{50}$	60%	0.5
0.9	0.75	0.45
50%	0.3	$\frac{1}{5}$

2 When written as a fraction, my denominator is a prime.
I am less than $\frac{2}{7}$.
I am not written in decimal form.

1	0.8	$\frac{1}{3}$
20%	$\frac{8}{9}$	40%
$\frac{1}{4}$	90%	0.3

ISBN: 9780170447379

Converting between decimals and percentages

Because percentages are out of 100,

- to change a decimal to a percentage, you **multiply by 100**
- to change a percentage to a decimal, you **divide by 100**.

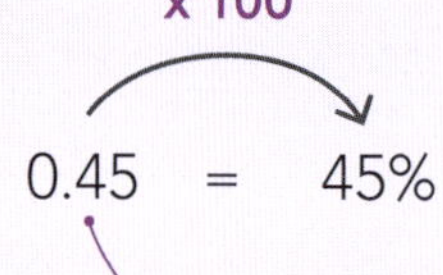

Examples: **1** x 100: 0.45 = 45%

Notice that **multiplying** by 100 is the same as moving the decimal point two places to the **right**.

2 ÷ 100: 73% = 0.73

Notice that **dividing** by 100 is the same as moving the decimal point two places to the **left**.

Convert the following decimals into percentages.

1 0.25 = ______________ **2** 0.40 = ______________

3 0.32 = ______________ **4** 0.69 = ______________

5 0.13 = ______________ **6** 0.99 = ______________

7 0.87 = ______________ **8** 0.11 = ______________

9 0.51 = ______________ **10** 0.75 = ______________

11 0.26 = ______________ **12** 0.09 = ______________

13 0.365 = ______________ **14** 0.03 = ______________

15 1.0 = ______________ **16** 1.2 = ______________

17 6 = ______________ **18** 1.34 = ______________

ISBN: 9780170447379

Convert the following percentages into decimals.

19 63% = ______________________ **20** 52% = ______________________

21 99% = ______________________ **22** 14% = ______________________

23 80% = ______________________ **24** 22% = ______________________

25 38% = ______________________ **26** 99% = ______________________

27 10% = ______________________ **28** 78% = ______________________

29 48.5% = ______________________ **30** 32.7% = ______________________

31 130% = ______________________ **32** 200% = ______________________

33 Every square below has one of a matching value except for one. Which is the odd one out?

10%	$\frac{3}{5}$	0.4	25%	$\frac{11}{20}$
60%	80%	$\frac{6}{8}$	100%	$\frac{7}{10}$
$\frac{4}{5}$	$\frac{1}{4}$	0.55	0.3	0.2
$\frac{1}{5}$	70%	$\frac{3}{25}$	$\frac{4}{10}$	0.75
$\frac{3}{10}$	0.12	$\frac{50}{50}$	0.5	$\frac{1}{10}$

ISBN: 9780170447379

Converting between fractions, decimals and percentages

Fill in the gaps.

	Fraction	Decimal	Percentage
1	$\frac{1}{2}$		
2			60%
3		0.2	
4	$\frac{1}{4}$		
5		0.4	
6	$\frac{4}{5}$		
7			35%
8		0.75	
9			30%
10	$\frac{7}{7}$		
11		0.375	
12	$\frac{1}{8}$		
13			55%
14		0.875	
15			110%

ISBN: 9780170447379

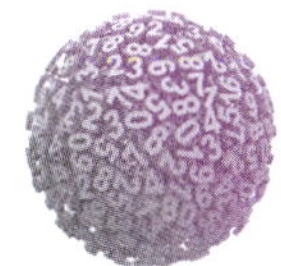

Challenge 4

Place the numbers in the list below in ascending order (smallest to largest).
Hint: Change them all to decimals first.

1

40%	$\frac{9}{20}$	0.35	~~30%~~	$\frac{4}{8}$	0.48	$\frac{23}{50}$	42%
			0.30				

Smallest | Largest

30%							

2

81%	$\frac{41}{50}$	0.86	79%	$\frac{4}{5}$	0.84	$\frac{17}{20}$	89%

Smallest | Largest

3

$\frac{3}{25}$	0.10	$\frac{7}{50}$	11%	0.13	$\frac{6}{40}$	0.16	10.5%

Smallest | Largest

4

65%	$\frac{5}{8}$	0.63	$\frac{16}{25}$	65.5%	0.654	$\frac{129}{200}$	0.66

Smallest | Largest

ISBN: 9780170447379

Calculating percentages

- Remember, 'percent' means out of 100, so turning a fraction into a percentage means **multiplying by 100**.

Example: There are 30 students in Annie's class, and **18** of them are boys. What percentage of the class are boys?

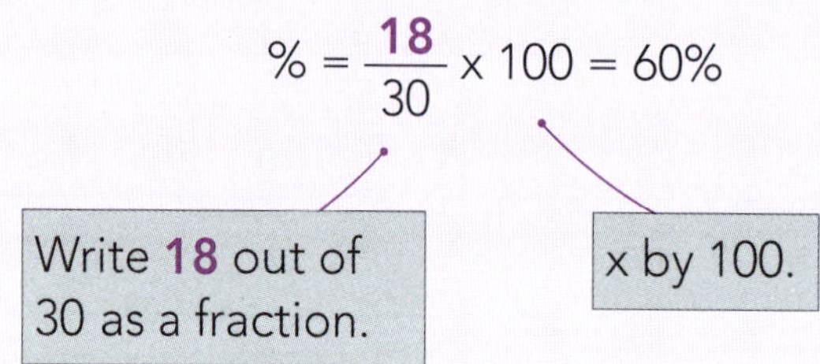

Write the following amounts as percentages.

1 68 out of 80 = ______
= ______

2 90 out of 125 = ______
= ______

3 12 out of 60 = ______
= ______

4 140 out of 1000 = ______
= ______

5 21 out of 30 = ______
= ______

6 7 out of 70 = ______
= ______

7 24 out of 96 = ______
= ______

8 96 out of 150 = ______
= ______

9 127 out of 200 = ______
= ______

10 1111 out of 5000 = ______
= ______

11 On Monday, 12 students were late to school. The school has a roll of 150 students. What percentage of students were late on Monday?

______

12 You have 206 bones in your body, and 52 of them are in your feet. What percentage of your bones are in your feet?

______

 ISBN: 9780170447379

Finding percentages of amounts

- There are many ways of doing this.

Examples:

1 Find 25% of 68.

You should be able to do this without a calculator.

Either: convert the percentage to a decimal: 25% **of** 68 = 0.25 **x** 68
= 17

Remember, '**of**' means **x**.

Or: convert the percentage to a fraction: 25% **of** 68 = $\frac{25}{100}$ **x** 68
= 17

- It is also possible to use the % button on your **calculator**.
- Not all calculators are the same, so you will need to experiment until you find how yours works. Two possibilities are shown in the box below.

2 Find 30% of $90.

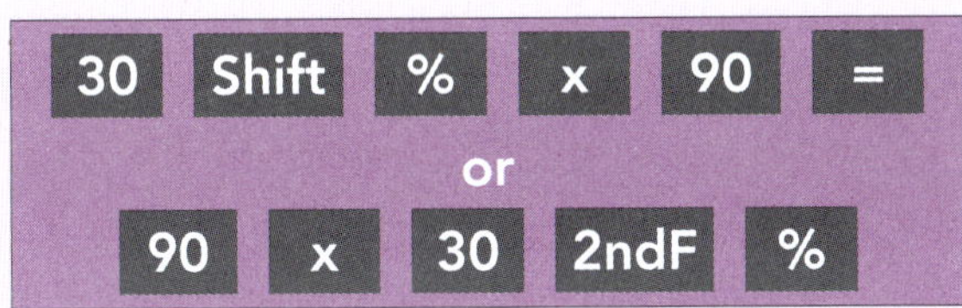

So, 30% of 90 = 27.

Calculate these.

1 10% of 40 = ______
= ______

2 20% of 45 = ______
= ______

3 25% of 300 = ______
= ______

4 80% of 650 = ______
= ______

5 65% of 460 = ______
= ______

6 12% of 850 = ______
= ______

7 3% of 1 100 = ______
= ______

8 25% of 800 000 = ______
= ______

ISBN: 9780170447379

9 15% of 940 = ____________________

10 18% of 1 200 = ____________________

11 55% of 26 = ____________________

12 24% of 8 200 = ____________________

13 94% of 110 = ____________________

14 12% of 560 = ____________________

15 2.5% of 3 600 = ____________________

16 2.8% of 500 000 = ____________________

17 In a group of 60 students, 95% can swim. How many students can swim?

____

18 In a survey of adults, 8% did not know how to ride a bike. If 450 adults were surveyed, how many could not ride a bike?

____

19 In a packet of lollies, 35% of them are red. If there are 40 lollies in the packet, how many are *not* red?

____

20 Get from the start of the maze to the finish by highlighting and passing through only the correct calculations. You may move horizontally or vertically but not diagonally.

Start

12% of 50 = 6	55% of 60 = 33	20% of 60 = 10	9% of 10 = 10	25% of 92 = 22	32% of 50 = 15	16% of 80 = 18.2
60% of 84 = 50	45% of 56 = 25.2	10% of 70 = 7	59% of 30 = 27	80% of 65 = 51	45% of 22 = 9	70% of 64 = 48
25% of 83 = 20.2	11% of 88 = 10	13% of 30 = 3.9	33% of 70 = 21	40% of 30 = 10	7% of 40 = 2	28% of 60 = 18
15% of 20 = 3	26% of 85 = 22.1	70% of 40 = 28	26% of 95 = 27.4	50% of 67 = 33.5	2% of 75 = 1.5	16% of 125 = 20
40% of 67 = 26.8	92% of 35 = 33	35% of 52 = 12.8	6% of 35 = 2.2	27% of 40 = 10.8	76% of 40 = 34	1% of 150 = 1.5
85% of 20 = 17	8% of 65 = 5.2	30% of 80 = 24	46% of 45 = 19	98% of 40 = 39.2	30% of 30 = 10	70% of 85 = 59.5
26% of 85 = 22.2	43% of 76 = 30	63% of 50 = 31.5	18% of 75 = 13.5	42% of 50 = 21	27% of 50 = 15	**90% of 90 = 81**

Finish

 ISBN: 9780170447379

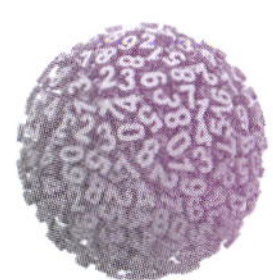

Mixing it up

1 Write down the value of the purple numeral as numbers and in words.

a 7 632 = ______________ **b** 23.16 = ______________

2 Calculate these.

a 19% of 250 = ______________ **b** 2% of 40 = ______________

3 Highlight the larger of these pairs.

a $\frac{4}{5}$ or $\frac{41}{50}$ **b** $\frac{7}{8}$ or 85%

c 0.45 or $\frac{11}{25}$ **d** 0.3 or $\frac{1}{3}$

4 Place these decimals in ascending order (smallest to largest).

2.13, 3.21, 3.12, 2.31 ________ ________ ________ ________

5 **a** What percentage is shaded purple? ______________

b What percentage is white? ______________

6 Write 62 853 using words. ______________

7 12.6 increased by four tenths = ______________

8 13 out of 20 people have a pet at home. What percentage is this? ______________

9 Write eight thousand, four hundred and twelve using numerals. ______________

10 Place the numbers in the list below in ascending order (smallest to largest).
Hint: Change them all to decimals first.

10%	$\frac{1}{5}$	0.13	15%	$\frac{3}{50}$	0.21	$\frac{3}{25}$	22%
			0.15				

Smallest Largest

ISBN: 9780170447379

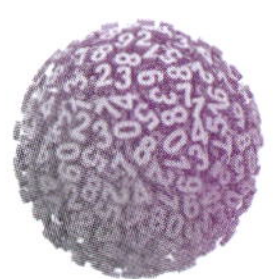

Word questions

1 Jennifer has 12 pens in her pencil case. She finds that 3 of them no longer work. What percentage of pens in her pencil case still work?

2 There are 18 shoes in the lost property, and 15 of them are school shoes. What fraction of them are not school shoes?

3 Would you rather have $\frac{3}{8}$ of a bag of 24 lollies or 25% of a bag of 40 lollies? Explain why.

4 Nikau had \$32 in his wallet, and he spent 85% of it on a present for his mother. How much money did he have left?

5 On Friday, $\frac{1}{8}$ of the class were playing rugby for the school and 37.5% of the class went to watch. If the class roll has 32 students, how many were in class that period?

6 A cake recipe requires $\frac{2}{5}$ of a cup of sugar and it also requires $\frac{2}{3}$ of a cup of sugar for the icing. How much sugar is required altogether? Write your answer as both an improper and a mixed fraction.

7 A chocolate bar has 24 squares. Bernie eats 25% of it and Charlie eats $\frac{3}{8}$. How many squares are left over?

8 A wildlife sanctuary has birds, mammals and reptiles. A quarter of the animals are birds and $\frac{2}{5}$ of the animals are mammals. What percentage are reptiles?

9 In a quiz, Jeremy got 21 questions correct out of 30. Lucy answered 16 out of 25 correctly. Who did better?

10 The weather forecaster said there was a 20% chance it would rain on any given day in the month of April. On how many days would you expect it to rain?

ISBN: 9780170447379

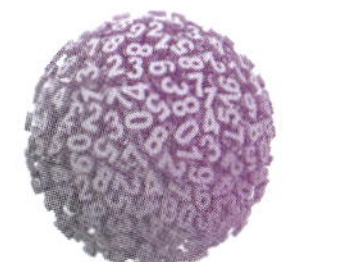

Rounding

- Often we need to round numbers to sensible and/or meaningful values.
- Never round until **after** you have completed your calculations.

Rounding to whole numbers

Locate the digit you have to round to. Is the digit to its **right** 5 or more?

Is it 5 or more?

No → Replace it and everything after it with 0s.

Yes → Increase the previous digit by one and replace everything after it with 0s.

Examples: **1** Round 786 to the nearest ten. — Is 786 closer to 780 or 790?

The tens digit is **8**. The digit to its right is **6**.
So 786 to the nearest ten = 790.

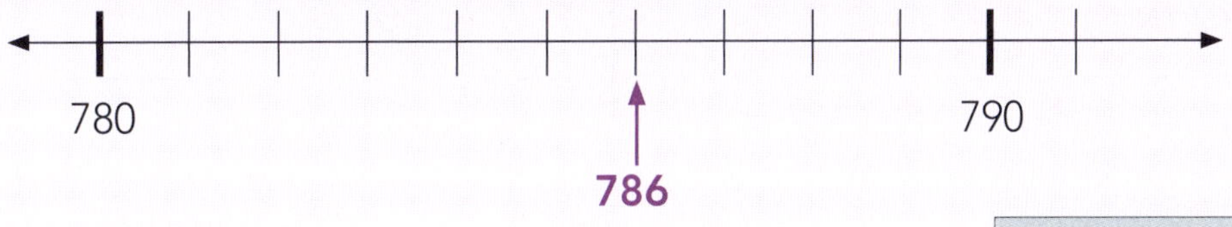

780 ... **786** ... 790

2 Round 1 549 to the nearest hundred. — Is 1 549 closer to 1 500 or 1 600?

The hundreds digit is **5**. The digit to its right is **4**.
So 1 549 to the nearest hundred = 1 500.

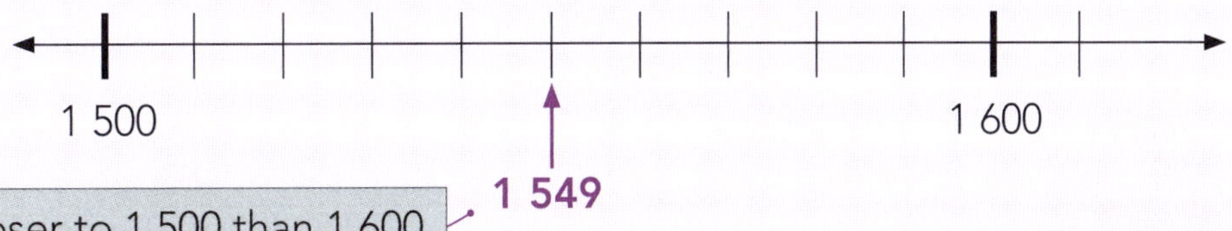

1 500 ... **1 549** ... 1 600

1 549 is closer to 1 500 than 1 600.

3 Round 17 500 to the nearest thousand. — Is 17 500 closer to 17 000 or 18 000?

The thousands digit is **7**. The digit to its right is **5**.
So 17 500 to the nearest thousand = 18 000.

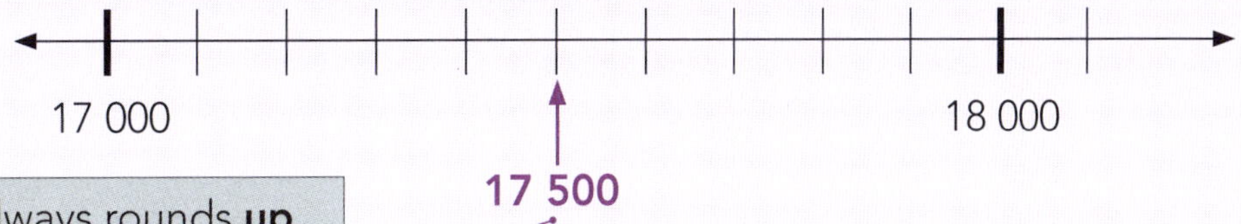

17 000 ... **17 500** ... 18 000

A **5** always rounds **up**.

More examples:

	Rounded to the nearest:	Last required digit	Answer
89	ten	**8**9	90
2 158	hundred	2 **1**58	2 200
311 463	thousand	31**1** 463	311 000
1 231 099	ten thousand	1 2**3**1 099	1 230 000
8 608 429	million	**8** 608 429	9 000 000

Complete these tables.

1

	Rounded to the nearest:	Last required digit	Answer
147	ten	1**4**7	
46 912	thousand	46 912	
9 251	hundred	9 251	
2 456 987	thousand	2 456 987	
987 215	ten	987 125	
53 143	hundred	53 143	

2

	Nearest ten	Nearest hundred	Nearest thousand
5 184	5 180	5 200	5 000
16 735			
221 264			
3 864			
28 612			
1 352 765			
685 555			

 ISBN: 9780170447379

Round these numbers to the nearest ten.

3 78 ______ **4** 932 ______

5 12 013 ______ **6** 74.9 ______

Round these numbers to the nearest hundred.

7 121 ______ **8** 34 276 ______

9 459 299 ______ **10** 8 032 855 ______

Round these numbers to the nearest thousand.

11 1 556 ______ **12** 18 190 ______

13 675 ______ **14** 125 645 ______

Round these numbers to the nearest ten thousand.

15 756 289 ______ **16** 75 061 238 ______

17 8 173 462 ______ **18** 11 562 ______

Round these numbers to the nearest million.

19 1 243 196 ______ **20** 2 652 222 ______

21 78 463 093 ______ **22** 99 991 992 ______

23 Complete the table.

Original number	Rounded to the nearest:	Rounded number
268		270
6 384		6 000
8 155		8 160
342 179		342 200
71 656		72 000
12 648 544		12 650 000
6 895		6 900
2 356 999		2 000 000

ISBN: 9780170447379

Rounding decimals

- The number of decimal places is the number of digits after the decimal point.

Examples:

Also known as rounded to the nearest tenth.

Number	9	9.**2**	9.25	9.256	9.256**0**
Number of decimal places	0	1	2	3	4

This is the same as rounding to the nearest whole number.

Notice that a **0** at the **end** counts as a decimal place.

- When asked to round to 1 dp (one decimal place), there should be **exactly** one digit after the decimal point.
- The process is similar to that for rounding to whole numbers.

Examples:

	Rounded to the nearest:	Last required digit	Answer
2.437	1 dp	2.**4**37	2.4
27.592	2 dp	27.5**9**2	27.59
142.8325	3 dp	142.83**2**5	142.833
0.82157	4 dp	0.821**5**7	0.8216

1 Complete the table.

	Rounded to how many dp?	Rounded number
3.568		3.57
24.567		24.6
412.03		412
0.3865		0.387
9.640		9.6
98.898		98.90
0.0023		0.002

 ISBN: 9780170447379

2 Complete the table.

	Rounded to the nearest:	Highlight the last required digit	Answer
38.541	1 dp	38.**5**41	
1.2678	3 dp	1.2678	
92.03541	4 dp	92.03541	
9.562	2 dp	9.562	
126.426	1 dp	126.426	
86.31	0 dp	86.31	
5.3288	3 dp	5.3288	
0.486	2 dp	0.486	

3 Complete the table.

	0 dp	1 dp	2 dp
5.67301			
12.5555		12.6	
6.6439	7		
0.9276			
1.0753			1.08
352.106	352		
0.01489			

4 Are these roundings correct or incorrect? If incorrect, round appropriately.

	Rounded to the nearest:	Answer	Correct or round appropriately
0.0635	1 dp	0.06	
50.4268	3 dp	50.427	
845.1249	2 dp	845.13	
0.003568	3 dp	0.0004	

ISBN: 9780170447379

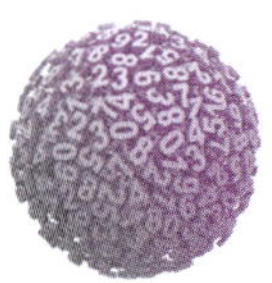

Estimations/approximations

- Sometimes an exact answer isn't necessary, so you can just estimate the answer.
- In order to estimate, round every number to **the nearest whole number**, and then do the calculations required.
- Don't forget to use BEDMAS.

Example: A list of prices:

This symbol means 'is approximately equal to'.

Oranges	\$3.99 ≈ \$4.00
Broccoli	\$2.29 ≈ \$2.00
Kumara	\$2.98 ≈ \$3.00

Round each value to the nearest dollar.

The approximate total is \$9.00.

$4 + 2 + 3 = 9$

Estimate the answers to the following. Do not use a calculator.

1 $1.31 + 5.87 =$ ______

2 $10.59 + 2.43 =$ ______

3 $15.26 - 8.09 =$ ______

4 $8.51 - 3.41 =$ ______

5 $28.30 + 1.13 + 4.2 =$ ______

______

6 $10.3 + 2.1 + 16.5 =$ ______

______

7 $13.21 + 4.67 - 2.94 =$

______

______

8 $14.6 - 5.2 + 1.12 =$

______

______

9 $2.4 \times 7.8 =$ ______

______

10 $15.4 \times 3.24 =$ ______

______

11 $\frac{20.16}{5.41} =$ ______

______

12 $15.76 \div 1.8 =$ ______

______

13 $9.43 \times 1.85 \div 2.6 =$ ______

______

14 $8.17 \div 2.03 \times 3.33 =$ ______

______

 ISBN: 9780170447379

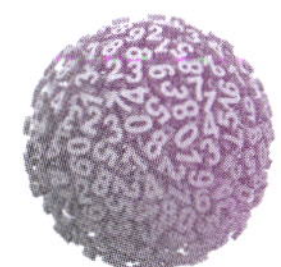

Challenge 5

1 Find a route from the start to the finish so that no two numbers along your route have the same value.

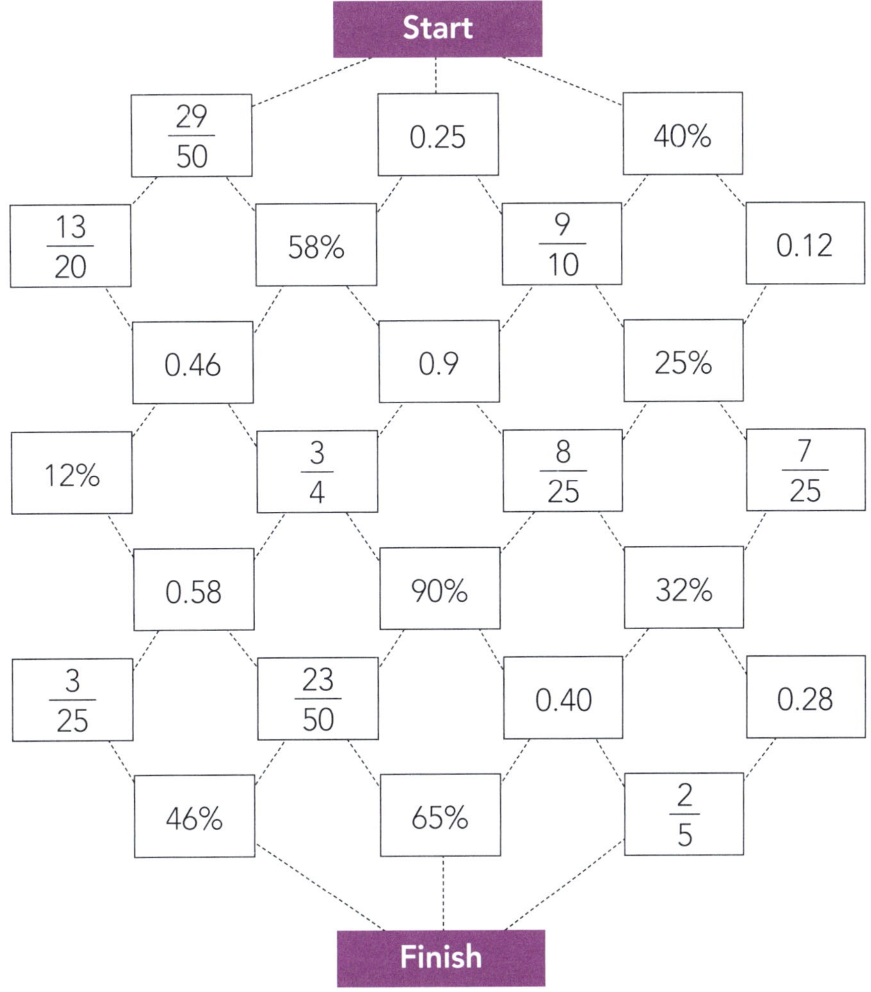

2 Fill the squares with a value. You may use each value only once.

27	16	60%
20	$\frac{2}{7}$	25
45	15	0.3
56	0.4	28
$\frac{4}{5}$	20%	70
40	50	8

	of		is	
	of		is	
	of		is	
	of		is	
	of		is	
	of		is	

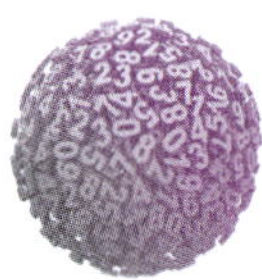

Revision 1

1 Use BEDMAS to calculate the following.

a $8 \times (3 + 1) - 13 =$ ______ b $\frac{8+6}{9-1} =$ ______

2 Is 31 a prime number and how do you know?

______

3 What is the lowest common multiple of 20 and 25? ______

4 What are the factors of 45? ______

5 Write the missing integers on the number line.

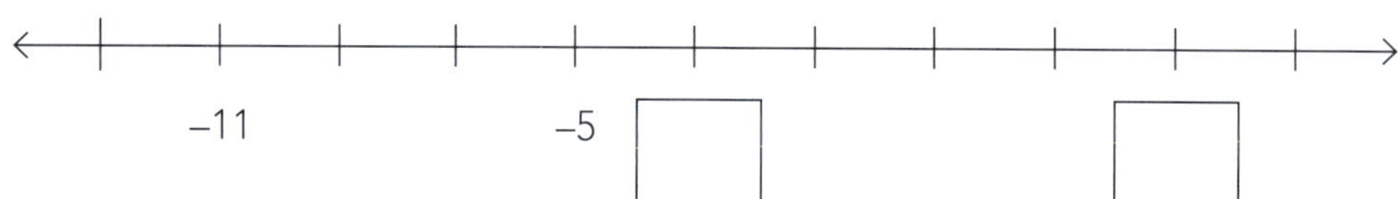

6 Calculate these.

a $2^4 =$ ______ b $\sqrt{121} =$ ______

c $3^3 \times 3^2 =$ ______ d $\sqrt[3]{125} =$ ______

7 Fill in the missing numbers to make these statements true.

a $\frac{9}{18} = \frac{1}{}$ b $\frac{17}{6} = 2\frac{}{6}$

c $\frac{}{5} = 2\frac{3}{5}$ d $\frac{}{11} = \frac{14}{22}$

8 Write a fraction equivalent to $\frac{2}{5}$. ______

9 Calculate these, simplifying where possible.

a $\frac{7}{8} - \frac{2}{8} =$ ______ b $\frac{1}{6} + \frac{4}{6} =$ ______

c $\frac{1}{5} \times \frac{2}{4} =$ ______ d $\frac{3}{4} \div \frac{2}{6} =$ ______

$=$ ______ $=$ ______

 ISBN: 9780170447379

10 Calculate these.

a $\frac{1}{7}$ of 84 = ______________

b $1\frac{1}{4}$ of 32 = ______________

11 Write the numbers using words.

a 12 921 ______________________

____

b 2.64 = ______________________

____

12 Write these numbers using numerals.

a Six hundred and thirty-two

____

b Eighty one thousand, five hundred and six

____

13 Highlight the larger value.

a $\frac{17}{25}$ $\frac{3}{5}$

b 0.83 $\frac{5}{6}$

c $\frac{4}{9}$ 45%

d 54% 0.545

14 Convert these values to fill in the gaps.

	Fraction	Decimal	Percentage
a	$\frac{3}{5}$		
b			35%
c		0.8	
d	$\frac{9}{8}$		

15 Calculate these.

a 12% of 106 = ______________

b 85% of 596 = ______________

16 Round these values appropriately.

	0 dp	1 dp	2 dp
6.5539			
439.1068			

ISBN: 9780170447379

17 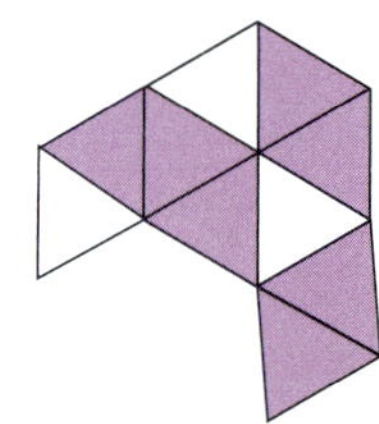

What fraction is:

shaded? ________

not shaded? ________

What percentage is:

shaded? ________

not shaded? ________

18 Write the missing decimals on the number line.

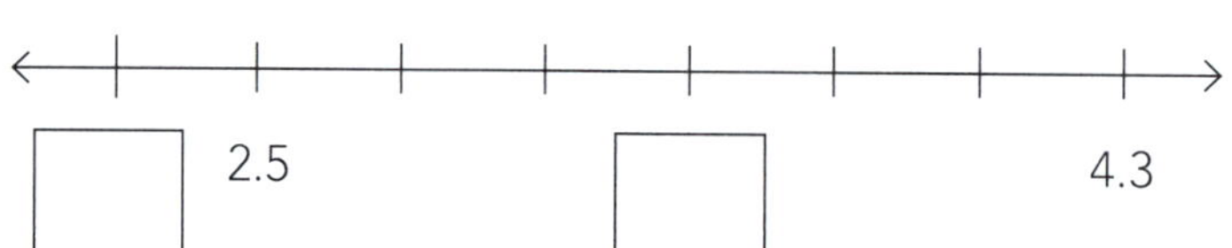

19 Round the following values appropriately.

	Nearest ten	Nearest hundred	Nearest thousand
1 936			
27 085			
745 689			

20 Place these decimals in ascending order (smallest to largest).

4.45, 5.54, 5.45, 4.54 ________ ________ ________ ________

21 Place the numbers in the list below in ascending order (smallest to largest).

80%	$\frac{5}{6}$	0.79	$\frac{39}{50}$	77%	0.81	$\frac{21}{25}$	75%

Smallest Largest

22 A garden has roses, lavender and daffodils in it. A third of the garden is daffodils and 25% are roses. What fraction of the garden is lavender?

____

23 Renee has to read a book for school. She has read two hundred and eighty-nine out of four hundred and twenty-five pages. What percentage does she have left to read?

____

 ISBN: 9780170447379

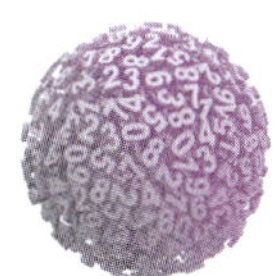

Revision 2

1 Use BEDMAS to calculate the following.

a $18 + (2 \times 1(5 + 1)) \div 4 =$ ______ **b** $\frac{4 \times 3}{2 + 2^2} =$ ______

2 Is 37 a prime number and how do you know?

______

3 What is the highest common factor of 24 and 36? ______

4 What are the first five multiples of 6? ______

5 Write the missing integers on the number line.

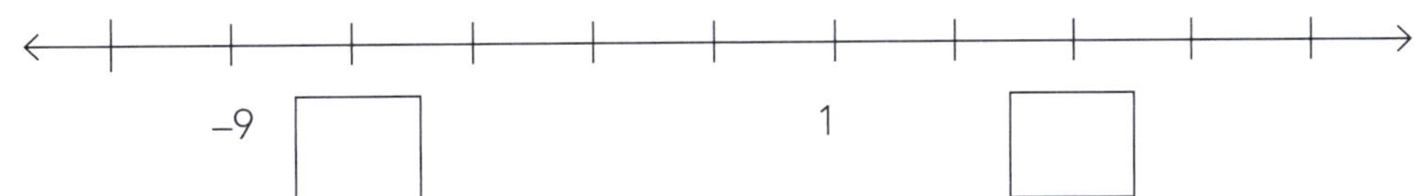

6 Calculate these.

a $3^3 =$ ______ **b** $\sqrt{64} =$ ______

c $2^3 \times 2^2 =$ ______ **d** $\sqrt[3]{216} =$ ______

7 Fill in the missing numbers to make these statements true.

a $\frac{4}{12} = \frac{1}{}$ **b** $\frac{23}{5} = 4\frac{}{5}$

c $\frac{}{6} = 1\frac{5}{6}$ **d** $\frac{}{3} = \frac{8}{24}$

8 Write a fraction equivalent to $\frac{2}{3}$. ______

9 Calculate these, simplifying where possible.

a $\frac{4}{5} - \frac{1}{5} =$ ______ **b** $\frac{1}{7} + \frac{4}{7} =$ ______

c $\frac{1}{4} \times \frac{2}{3} =$ ______ **d** $\frac{5}{6} \div \frac{2}{5} =$ ______

$=$ ______ $=$ ______

ISBN: 9780170447379

10 Calculate these.

a $\frac{2}{5}$ of 62 = ____________

b $1\frac{1}{3}$ of 33 = ____________

11 Write the numbers using words.

a 9 154 = ____________________

____

b 0.23 = ____________________

____

12 Write these numbers using numerals.

a Four hundred and eight-three

____

b Fifty-three thousand, four hundred and two

____

13 Highlight the larger value.

a $\frac{13}{20}$ $\frac{2}{3}$

b 0.62 $\frac{3}{5}$

c $\frac{2}{7}$ 29%

d 23% 0.2314

14 Convert these values to fill in the gaps.

	Fraction	Decimal	Percentage
a	$\frac{1}{5}$		
b		0.9	
c			25%
d		1.2	

15 Calculate these.

a 10% of 83 = ____________

b 55% of 362 = ____________

16 Round these values appropriately.

	0 dp	1 dp	2 dp
1.3468			
964.0561			

ISBN: 9780170447379

17 What fraction is:

shaded? ________

not shaded? ________

What percentage is:

shaded? ________

not shaded? ________

18 Write the missing decimals on the number line.

☐ 1.2 ☐ 2.8 ☐

19 Round the following values appropriately.

	Nearest ten	Nearest hundred	Nearest thousand
3 647			
12 876			
684 023			

20 Place these decimals in ascending order (smallest to largest).

9.80, 8.09, 8.90, 9.08 ________ ________ ________ ________

21 Place the numbers in the list below in ascending order (smallest to largest).

20%	$\frac{1}{4}$	0.30	$\frac{13}{50}$	19%	0.21	$\frac{6}{25}$	27%

Smallest Largest

22 A mobile vendor sells chocolate, vanilla and strawberry milkshakes. Half of the milkshakes it sells are chocolate and 30% of them are strawberry. What fraction is vanilla?

____

23 A walking track is 8 km long, and Joseph has walked 5 km of it. What percentage does he have left to walk?

____

ISBN: 9780170447379

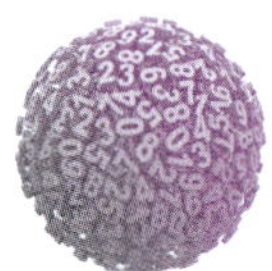

Answers

The language of mathematics (p. 6)

1 +
2 x
3 –
4 x
5 –
6 ÷
7 –
8 +
9 +
10 ÷
11 +
12 +
13 –
14 +
15 –
16 x
17 –
18 –
19 x
20 +

Integers (pp. 7–10)

Adding and subtracting (pp. 7–8)

1 5

2 –6

3 –5

4 3

5 7

6 –3

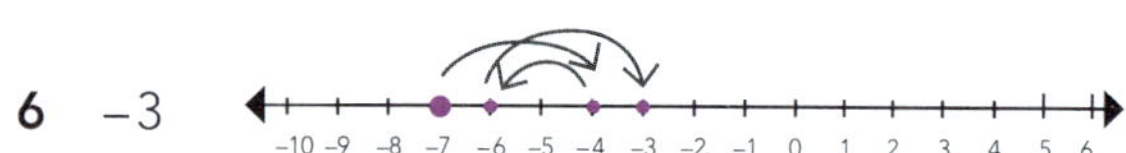

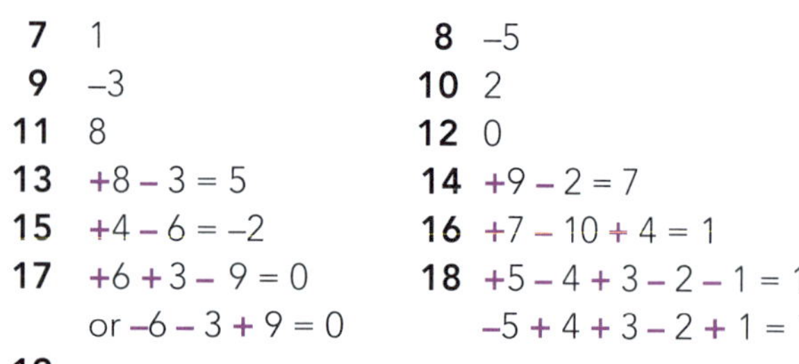

7 1
8 –5
9 –3
10 2
11 8
12 0
13 +8 – 3 = 5
14 +9 – 2 = 7
15 +4 – 6 = –2
16 +7 – 10 + 4 = 1
17 +6 + 3 – 9 = 0
or –6 – 3 + 9 = 0
18 +5 – 4 + 3 – 2 – 1 = 1
–5 + 4 + 3 – 2 + 1 = 1

19

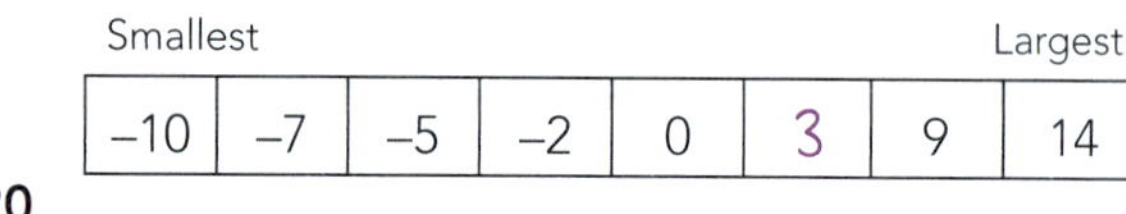

Smallest → Largest

–10	–7	–5	–2	0	3	9	14

20

Smallest → Largest

–9	–8	–4	–2	–1	2	6	8

21

Smallest → Largest

–21	–12	–2	–1	1	2	12	21

Integers on number lines (pp. 9–10)

1

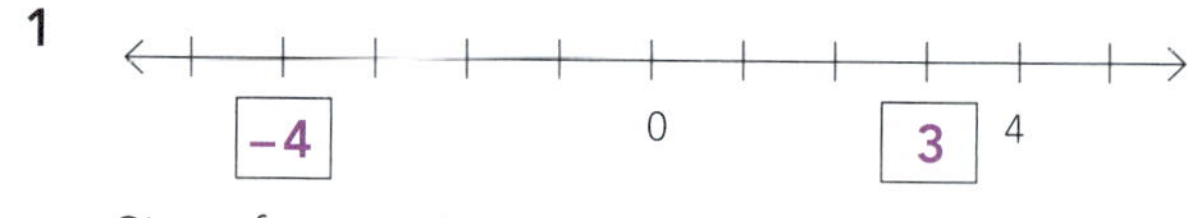

Size of gap = 1

2

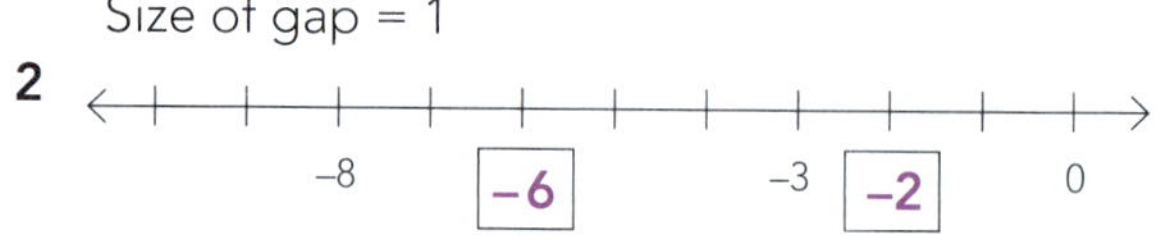

Size of gap = $\frac{-8 - -3}{5} = -1$

3

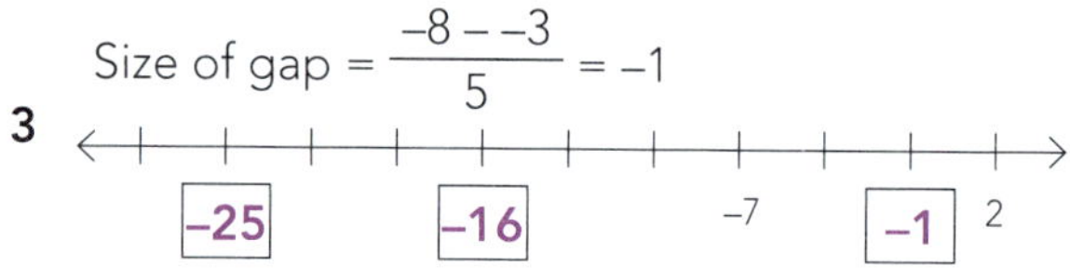

Size of gap = $\frac{-7 - 2}{3} = -3$

4

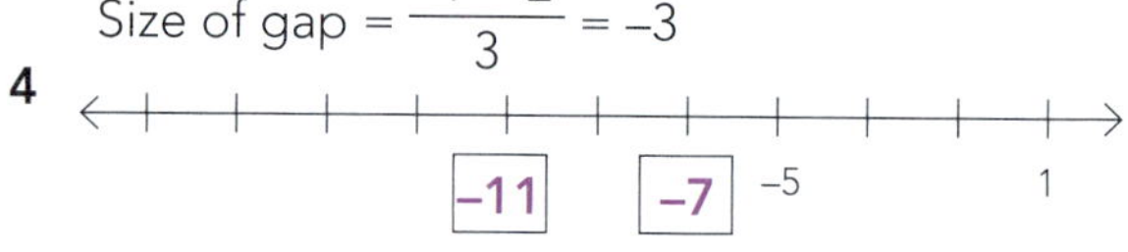

Size of gap = $\frac{-5 - 1}{3} = -2$

5

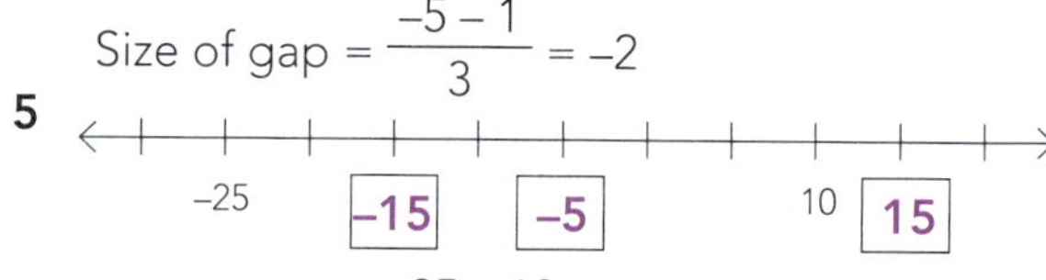

Size of gap = $\frac{-25 - 10}{7} = -5$

6

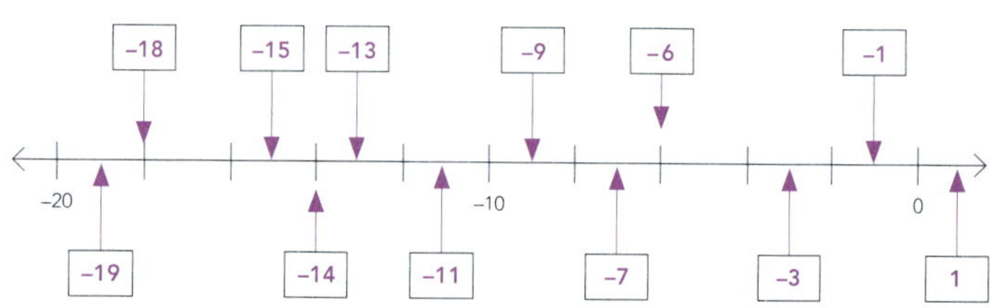

Challenge 1 (p. 10)

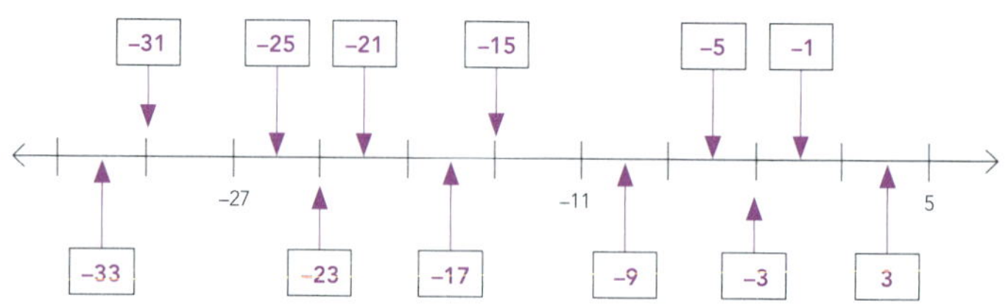

Multiplying and dividing (p. 11)

1 12
2 –3
3 –9
4 3
5 –20
6 –4
7 –12
8 2
9 21
10 –3
11 –9
12 4
13 2
14 3
15 –5
16 2
17 –20
18 –4

 ISBN: 9780170447379

Types of numbers (pp. 12–20)

Multiples (pp. 12–13)

1

Number	First five multiples
2	2, 4, 6, 8, 10
3	3, 6, 9, 12, 15
6	6, 12, 18, 24, 30
4	4, 8, 12, 16, 20
10	10, 20, 30, 40, 50
9	9, 18, 27, 36, 45
11	11, 22, 33, 44, 55
7	7, 14, 21, 28, 35
20	20, 40, 60, 80, 100
5	5, 10, 15, 20, 25
1	1, 2, 3, 4, 5
8	8, 16, 24, 32, 40

2

True or False
True
True
False
True
False
False
True
True
False
True
True
False

3

Start

66	**42**	16	62	**78**	**54**	**30**
82	**12**	64	**72**	**60**	22	**114**
18	**108**	26	**132**	28	38	**126**
48	46	**84**	**36**	104	10	**90**
96	**24**	**120**	14	76	68	**102**

Finish

4 3, 6, 9, **12**, 15
4, 8, **12** LCM = 12

5 2, 4, 6, 8, **10**
5, **10** LCM = 10

6 6, 12, 18, **24**, 30
8, 16, **24** LCM = 24

7 3, 6, 9, 12, **15**
5, 10, **15** LCM = 15

8 6, 12, 18, 24, **30**
15, **30** LCM = 30

9 10, 20, 30, 40, 50, **60**
12, 24, 36, 48, **60** LCM = 60

10 Jo 4, 8, **12**, 16, 20, 24, 28
Chrystal 6, **12**
In 12 minutes they will complete a lap together.

Factors (pp. 14–15)

1

Number	Factors
10	1, 2, 5, 10
14	1, 2, 7, 14
18	1, 2, 3, 6, 9, 18
21	1, 3, 7, 21
9	1, 3, 9
15	1, 3, 5, 15
6	1, 2, 3, 6
20	1, 2, 4, 5, 10, 20
11	1, 11
30	1, 2, 3, 5, 6, 10, 15, 30
24	1, 2, 3, 4, 6, 8, 12, 24
100	1, 2, 4, 5, 10, 20, 25, 50, 100

2

True or False
False
True
False
True
False
False
True
True
False
True
True
False

3

Start

10	7	25	9	17	22	39
5	**15**	**1**	**6**	13	42	27
14	23	8	**2**	32	38	19
11	24	31	**30**	**10**	**12**	33
21	0	45	16	28	**4**	**60**

Finish

4 1, 3, **5**, 15
1, 2, 4, **5**, 10, 20 HCF = 5

5 1, 2, 3, **6**
1, 2, 3, 4, **6**, 12 HCF = 6

6 1, **2**, 5, 10
1, **2**, 3, 4, 6, 8, 12, 24 HCF = 2

7 1, 2, 3, 5, 6, **10**, 15, 30
1, 2, 4, 5, 8, **10**, 20, 40 HCF = 10

8 1, **11**
1, 2, **11**, 22 HCF = 11

9 1, 3, **9**, 27
1, 3, 7, **9**, 21, 63 HCF = 9

10 She could have **8** groups with **2** girls and **1** boy in each group.
She could have **4** groups with **4** girls and **2** boys in each group.
She could have **2** groups with **8** girls and **4** boy in each group.

ISBN: 9780170447379

Prime numbers (pp. 16–18)

1

1	**2**	**3**	4	**5**	6	**7**	8	9	10
11	12	**13**	14	15	16	**17**	18	**19**	20
21	22	**23**	24	25	26	27	28	**29**	30
31	32	33	34	35	36	**37**	38	39	40

2 41

3 All prime numbers are odd except for 2.

4 13 + 11 = 24
19 + 5 = 24
17 + 7 = 24

Prime factors (pp. 16–18)

5 $16 = 2^4$

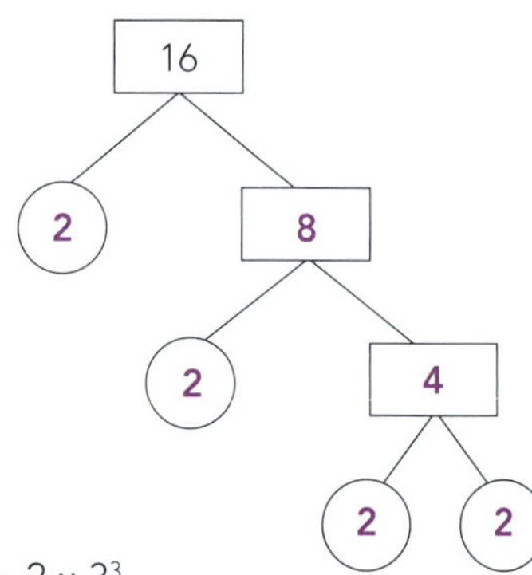

6 $54 = 2 \times 3^3$

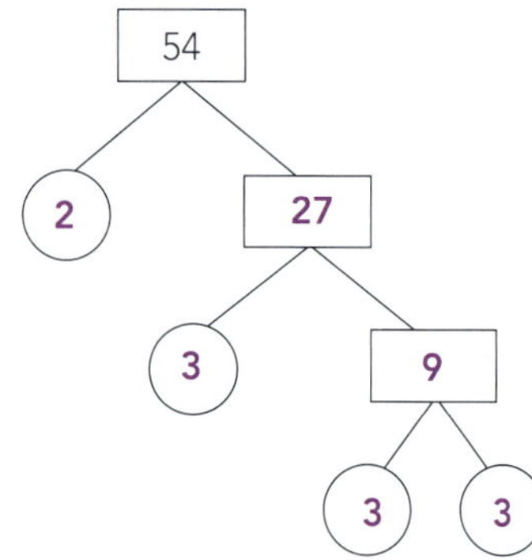

7 $32 = 2^5$

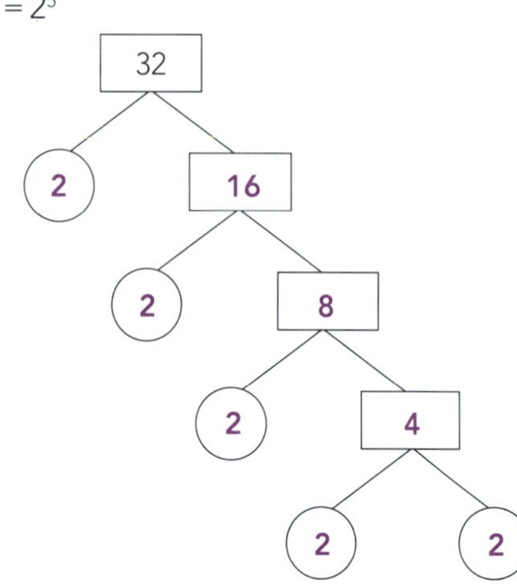

8 $72 = 2^3 \times 3^2$

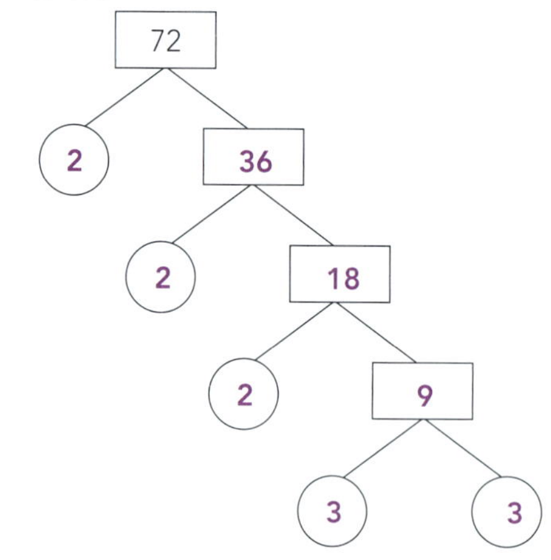

9 $75 = 3 \times 5^2$

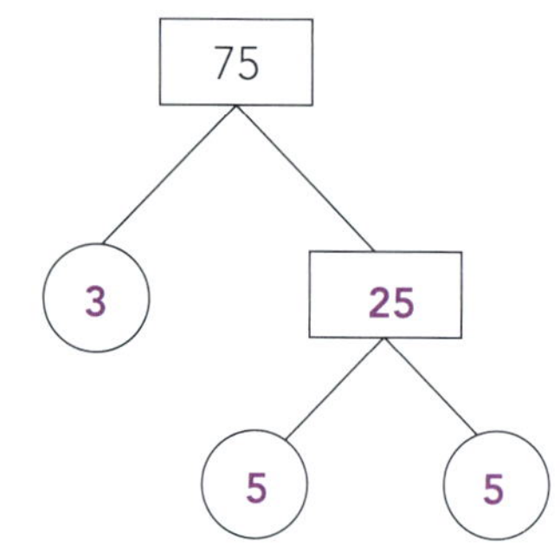

10 $117 = 3^2 \times 13$

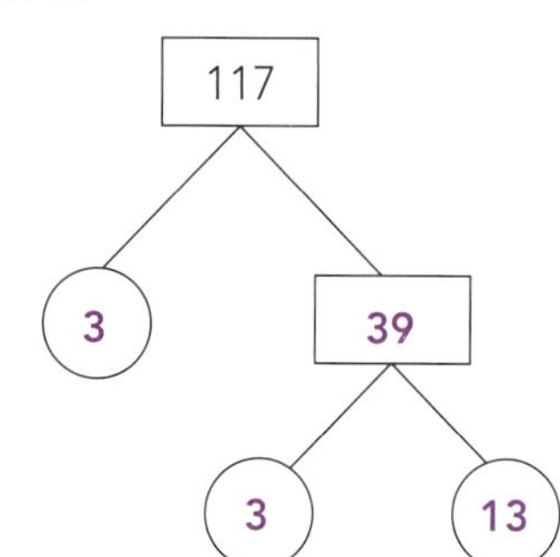

11 $840 = 2^3 \times 3 \times 5 \times 7$

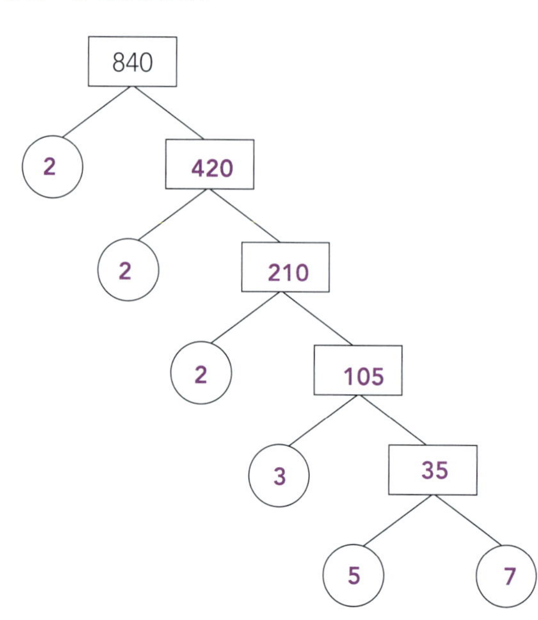

ISBN: 9780170447379

12 $1\,092 = 2^2 \times 3 \times 7 \times 13$

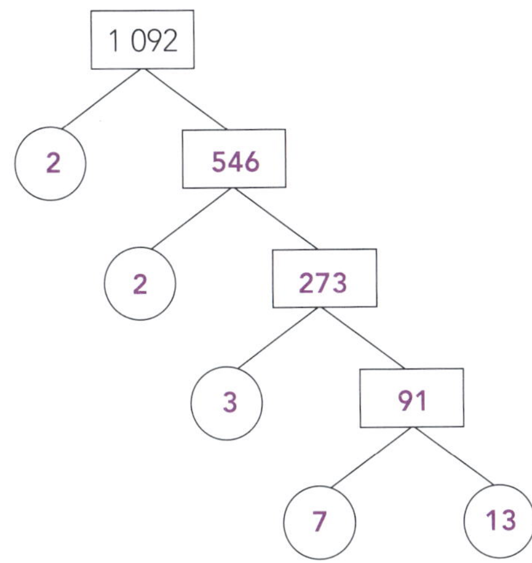

13 $140 = 2^2 \times 5 \times 7$

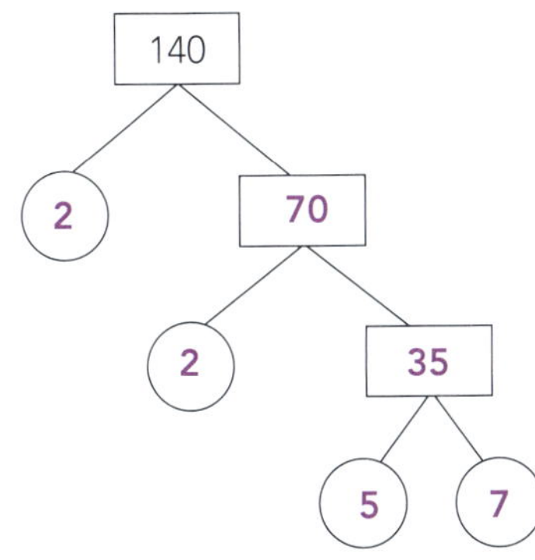

14 $147 = 3 \times 7^2$

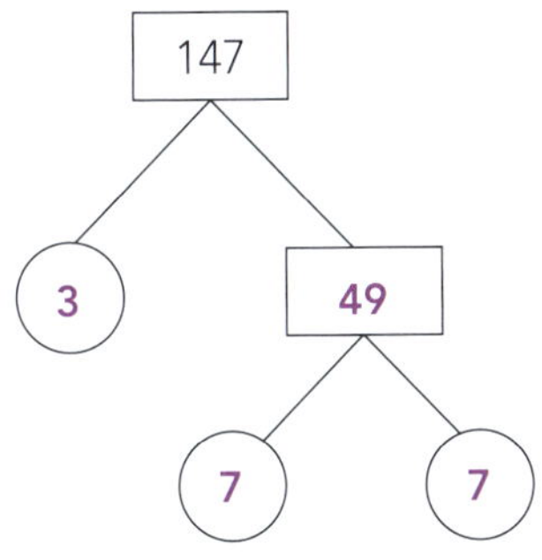

Square numbers (pp. 19–20)

1

Square number	Picture	Notation
1	●	1^2
4	● ● ● ●	2^2
9	● ● ● ● ● ● ● ● ●	3^2
16	● ● ● ● ● ● ● ● ● ● ● ● ● ● ● ●	4^2
25	● ●	5^2
36	● ●	6^2

Powers (pp. 20–21)

1 4^5
2 6^2
3 5^3
4 9^4
5 8^1
6 3^3
7 2^2
8 1^1 or anything ^{0}
9 $2 \times 2 \times 2 \times 2 \times 2 = 32$
10 $4 \times 4 \times 4 = 64$
11 $9 \times 9 = 81$
12 $8 \times 8 \times 8 \times 8 = 4\,096$
13 $7 \times 7 \times 7 = 343$
14 10
15 $5 \times 5 \times 5 \times 5 \times 5 \times 5 = 15\,625$
16 1
17 $3 \times 3 \times 3 \times 3 \times 3 = 243$
18 $3 \times 3 \times 3 \times 3 \times 3 = 243$
19 Yes; 5
20 33
21 1 015
22 144
23 4
24 8
25 1 021
26 0.09
27 0.5
28 25
29 625
30 –125
31 125
32 $\frac{1}{5}$
33 5
34 1
35 15 625
36 3 125
37 $\frac{1}{25}$

Roots (p. 22)

1 3
2 5
3 7
4 9
5 2
6 6
7 10
8 6
9 2
10 3
11 2
12 0.5

ISBN: 9780170447379

Order of operations (pp. 23–29)

B	Brackets
E	Exponents
D	Division
M	Multiplication
A	Addition
S	Subtraction

1 4 **2** 3
3 10 **4** 18
5 17 **6** 9
7 1 **8** 0
9 9 **10** 6
11 7 **12** 25
13 18 **14** –8
15 7 **16** 6
17 2 **18** 4

19
⚡ = 6 ☾ = 2
18

20
★ = 4 ♣ = 2
0

Words to calculations (p. 25)

1 (14 + 4) ÷ 2 = $9
2 ((14 x 2) + 2) ÷ 2 = $15
3 14 – 2 + 4 = 16
4 $\frac{(14-4)}{2}$ = $5
5 $\frac{14}{2} + 4$ = $11
6 (14 x 2) – 4 = $24
7 (14 + 4) x 2 = $36
8 $\frac{(14-2)}{4}$ = $3

Using your calculator (pp. 26–27)

The muster

Bobbie and **Ollie** sat on the **big log** waiting for the **billies** to **boil**. The sun was going down. It would be hard to **see** soon. **Bob's** leg kicked out at the **soil**, shaking his boot **loose**. He was desperate to lie down and sleep but felt **ill** with hunger, the **bile** rising up. The pan began to **sizzle** as **Ollie** put the **eel** in. **Oil** oozed out of the **gill** cut. He cracked the **eggs** and they began to **gloss** over as they cooked. There was nothing else. **Ollie** began to **ogle** the food. **Ollie** passed **Bobbie** the plate. They began to **gobble** the food down. **Bob** would **oblige** by cleaning the plates. They lay down to sleep. The **soles** of his feet hurt, his **legs** ached, his arm itched where he had been stung by a **bee** but he was not hungry any more. They had the steers down. The muster was nearly done.

Mixing it up (p. 28)

1 1, 2, 3, 6, 9, 18 **2** Yes; 93 ÷ 3 = 31.
3 **a** 10 **b** 7
4 **a** 6 **b** 8
5 –18, –12, –4
6 **a** No; it is divisible by 3, 7, 9 and 21.
b $88 = 2^3 \times 11$

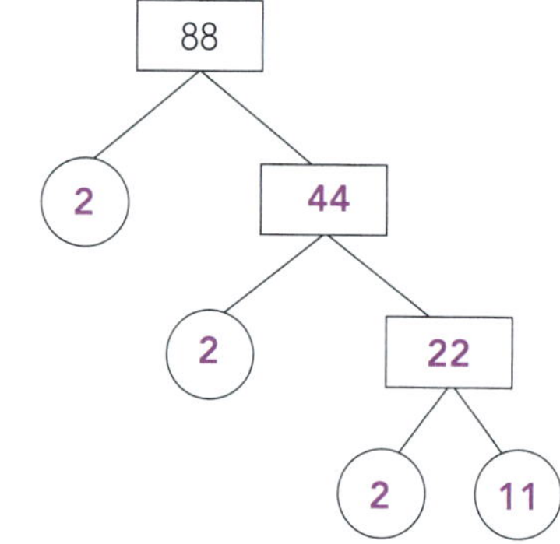

c 2
7 **a** 8 **b** 64
8 49 **9** 6

Fractions (pp. 29–49)

Shading fractions (pp. 29–30)

1	Shaded	$\frac{2}{4}$	**2**	Shaded	$\frac{3}{7}$
	Not shaded	$\frac{2}{4}$		Not shaded	$\frac{4}{7}$
3	Shaded	$\frac{4}{6}$	**4**	Shaded	$\frac{5}{8}$
	Not shaded	$\frac{2}{6}$		Not shaded	$\frac{3}{8}$
5	Shaded	$\frac{1}{4}$	**6**	Shaded	$\frac{6}{10}$
	Not shaded	$\frac{3}{4}$		Not shaded	$\frac{4}{10}$
7	Shaded	$\frac{4}{5}$	**8**	Shaded	$\frac{3}{6}$
	Not shaded	$\frac{1}{5}$		Not shaded	$\frac{3}{6}$
9	Shaded	$\frac{2}{5}$	**10**	Shaded	$\frac{5}{7}$
	Not shaded	$\frac{3}{5}$		Not shaded	$\frac{2}{7}$

11 They add to 1.

ISBN: 9780170447379

12
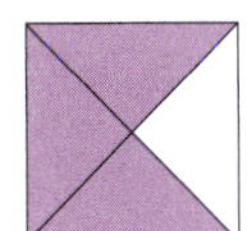

13
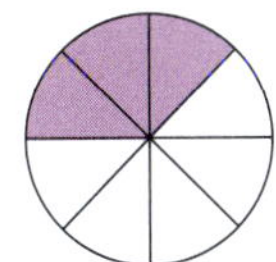

14
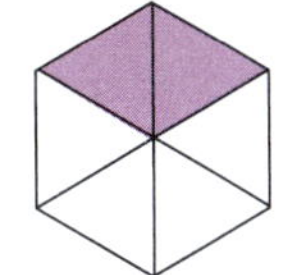

15

16
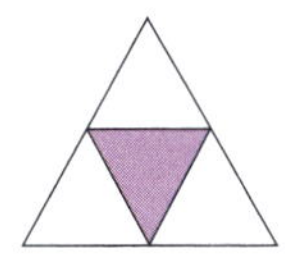

17
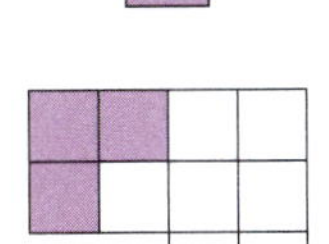

18
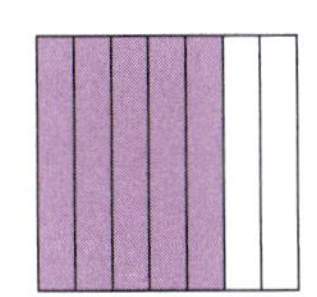

19
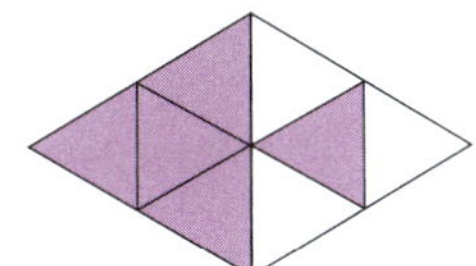

20
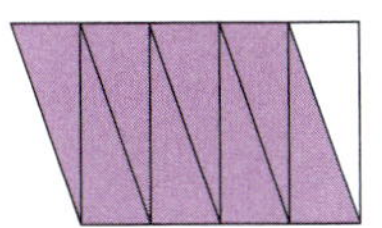

21
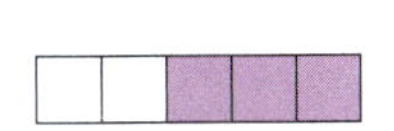

22
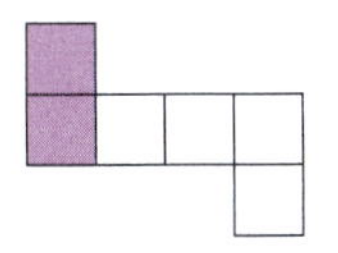

23

24
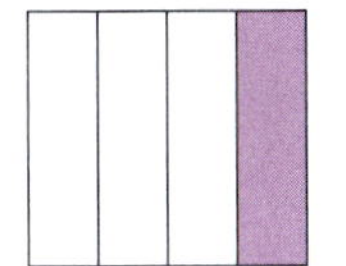

25
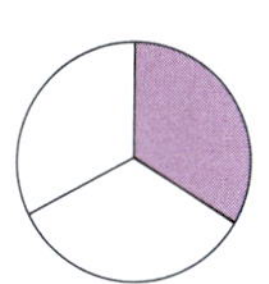

Numerators and denominators (pp. 31–32)

1 $\frac{1}{5}$ $\frac{2}{5}$

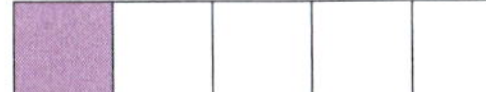

When the **numerator** increases, the size of the shaded section **increases**.

2 $\frac{1}{3}$ $\frac{1}{4}$

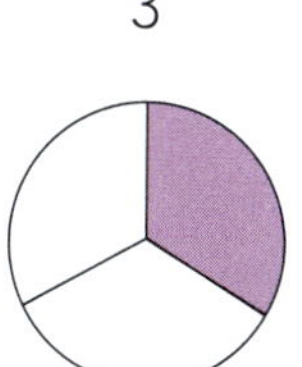

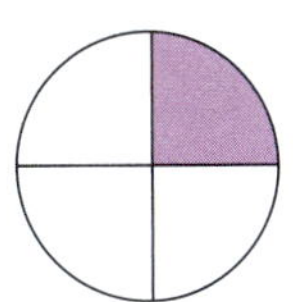

When the **denominator** increases, the size of the shaded section **decreases**.

3 $\frac{4}{6}$ $\frac{5}{6}$

4 $\frac{3}{4}$ $\frac{2}{4}$

5 $\frac{1}{5}$ $\frac{1}{4}$

6 $\frac{1}{7}$ $\frac{1}{8}$

7 $\frac{1}{5}$ $\frac{2}{5}$

8 $\frac{1}{7}$ $\frac{1}{5}$

9 $\frac{9}{10}$ $\frac{7}{10}$

10 $\frac{3}{9}$ $\frac{3}{8}$

11 a

$\frac{1}{6}$ $\frac{4}{6}$ $\frac{2}{6}$ $\frac{5}{6}$ $\frac{6}{6}$ $\frac{3}{6}$

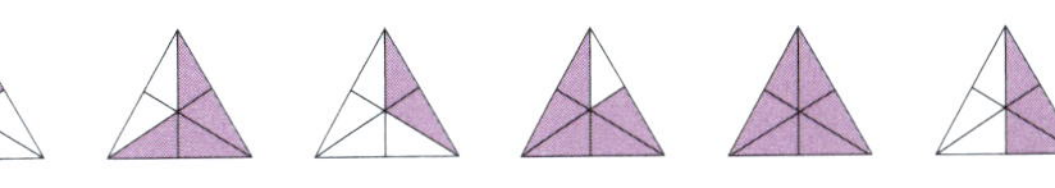

b

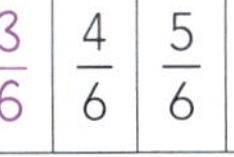

Smallest	$\frac{1}{6}$	$\frac{2}{6}$	$\frac{3}{6}$	$\frac{4}{6}$	$\frac{5}{6}$	$\frac{6}{6}$	Largest

12 a

$\frac{1}{5}$ $\frac{1}{1}$ $\frac{1}{3}$ $\frac{1}{6}$ $\frac{1}{4}$ $\frac{1}{2}$

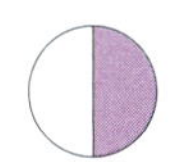

b

Smallest	$\frac{1}{6}$	$\frac{1}{5}$	$\frac{1}{4}$	$\frac{1}{3}$	$\frac{1}{2}$	$\frac{1}{1}$	Largest

Equivalent fractions (pp. 33–34)

1
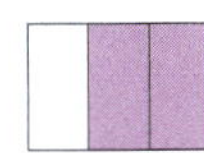
$\frac{4}{6} = \frac{2}{3}$

2
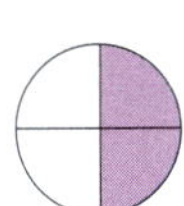
$\frac{4}{8} = \frac{2}{4}$

3
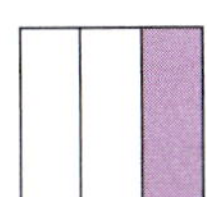
$\frac{3}{9} = \frac{1}{3}$

4
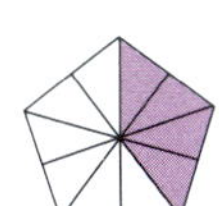
$\frac{2}{5} = \frac{4}{10}$

5
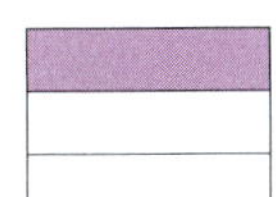
$\frac{4}{12} = \frac{1}{3}$

6
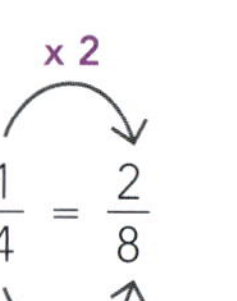
$\frac{1}{4} = \frac{2}{8}$ (× 2 top and bottom)

7
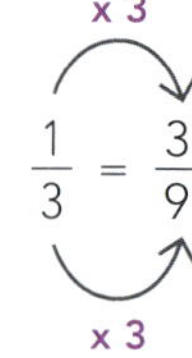
$\frac{1}{3} = \frac{3}{9}$ (× 3 top and bottom)

8
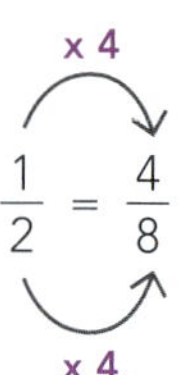
$\frac{1}{2} = \frac{4}{8}$ (× 4 top and bottom)

9
$\frac{2}{3} = \frac{8}{12}$ (× 4 top and bottom)

10
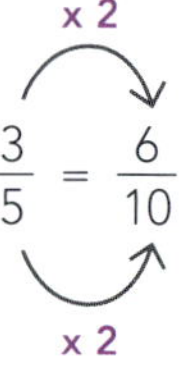
$\frac{3}{5} = \frac{6}{10}$ (× 2 top and bottom)

11
$\frac{1}{3} = \frac{3}{9}$ (× 3 top and bottom)

12
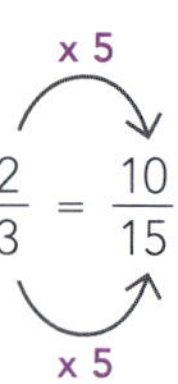
$\frac{2}{3} = \frac{10}{15}$ (× 5 top and bottom)

13
$\frac{1}{4} = \frac{3}{12}$ (× 3 top and bottom)

14 $\frac{1}{5} = \frac{2}{10} = \frac{3}{15} = \frac{4}{20} = \frac{5}{25} = \frac{6}{30} = \frac{7}{35}$

Simplifying fractions (p. 35)

1
$\frac{18}{20} = \frac{9}{10}$ (÷ 2 top and bottom)

2
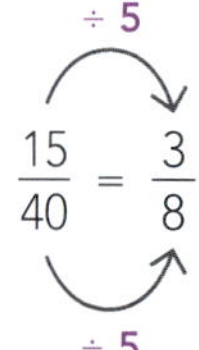
$\frac{15}{40} = \frac{3}{8}$ (÷ 5 top and bottom)

3
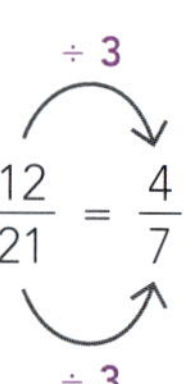
$\frac{12}{21} = \frac{4}{7}$ (÷ 3 top and bottom)

4
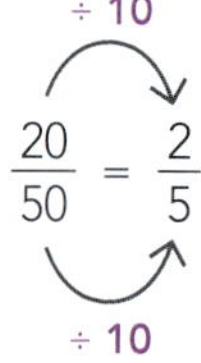
$\frac{20}{50} = \frac{2}{5}$ (÷ 10 top and bottom)

5 $\frac{15}{24} = \frac{5}{8}$

6 $\frac{33}{36} = \frac{11}{12}$

7 $\frac{3}{21} = \frac{1}{7}$

8 $\frac{16}{32} = \frac{1}{2}$

Comparing fractions (pp. 36–39)

1 $\frac{5}{6}$ $\frac{3}{4}$

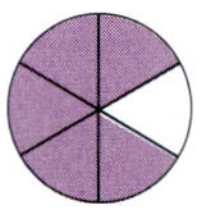
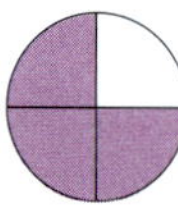

Larger Smaller

2 $\frac{3}{7}$ $\frac{2}{5}$

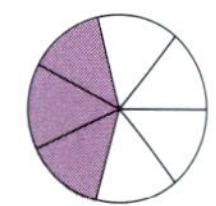

Larger Smaller

3 $\frac{3}{5}$ $\frac{2}{3}$

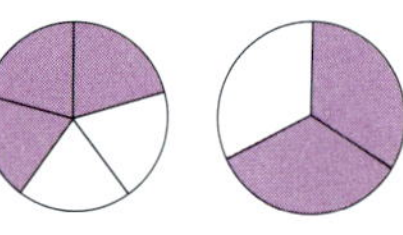

Smaller Larger

4 $\frac{2}{9}$ $\frac{1}{4}$

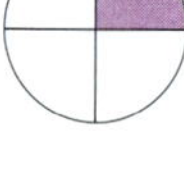

Smaller Larger

5 $\frac{4}{9}$ $\frac{3}{7}$

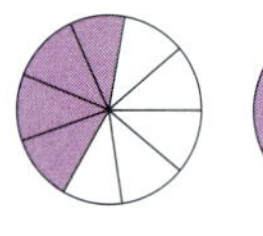

Larger Smaller

6 $\frac{3}{8}$ $\frac{4}{10}$

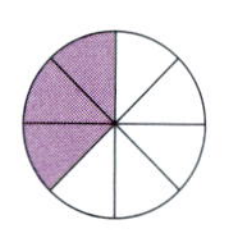
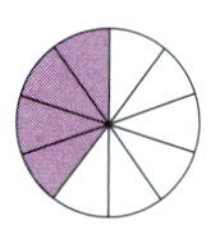

Smaller Larger

7 a $\frac{2}{3}$

$\frac{5}{8}$

$\frac{3}{4}$

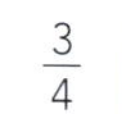
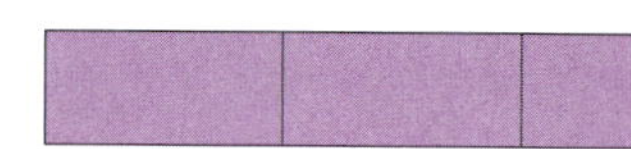

b Largest $\frac{3}{4}$ $\frac{2}{3}$ $\frac{5}{8}$ Smallest

8 a $\frac{2}{6}$

$\frac{3}{12}$

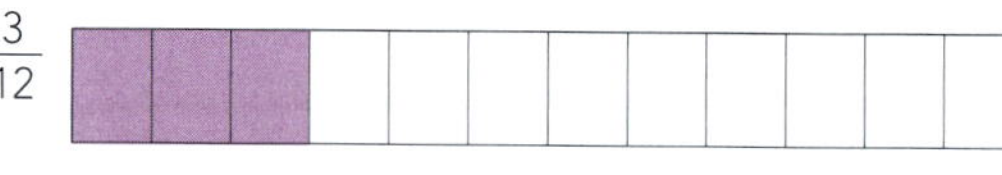

$\frac{4}{9}$

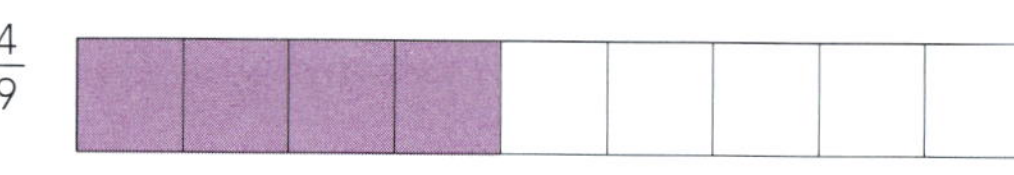

b Largest $\frac{4}{9}$ $\frac{2}{6}$ $\frac{3}{12}$ Smallest

9

	Method 1	Method 2
a	$\frac{1}{3}$ $\frac{2}{5}$ The larger fraction is $\frac{2}{5}$.	$\frac{1}{3} = \frac{5}{15}$ (× 5 top and bottom) $\frac{2}{5} = \frac{6}{15}$ (× 3 top and bottom)

 ISBN: 9780170447379

	Method 1	Method 2
b	$\frac{4}{7}$ $\frac{3}{5}$ The larger fraction is $\frac{3}{5}$.	$\frac{4}{7} = \frac{20}{35}$ (× 5) $\frac{3}{5} = \frac{21}{35}$ (× 7)
c	$\frac{3}{10}$ $\frac{1}{3}$ The larger fraction is $\frac{1}{3}$.	$\frac{3}{10} = \frac{9}{30}$ (× 3) $\frac{1}{3} = \frac{10}{30}$ (× 10)
d	$\frac{3}{5}$ $\frac{2}{3}$ The larger fraction is $\frac{2}{3}$.	$\frac{3}{5} = \frac{9}{15}$ (× 3) $\frac{2}{3} = \frac{10}{15}$ (× 5)
e	$\frac{3}{8}$ $\frac{1}{3}$ The larger fraction is $\frac{3}{8}$.	$\frac{3}{8} = \frac{9}{24}$ (× 3) $\frac{1}{3} = \frac{8}{24}$ (× 8)
f	$\frac{4}{5}$ $\frac{5}{6}$ The larger fraction is $\frac{5}{6}$.	$\frac{4}{5} = \frac{24}{30}$ (× 6) $\frac{5}{6} = \frac{25}{30}$ (× 5)

Converting between improper and mixed fractions (pp. 40–41)

	Improper fraction		Mixed fraction	
2	$\frac{7}{4}$	Seven quarters	$1\frac{3}{4}$	One and three quarters
3	$\frac{15}{9}$	Fifteen ninths	$1\frac{6}{9}$	One and six ninths
4	$\frac{10}{4}$	Ten quarters	$2\frac{2}{4}$	Two and two quarters

5 $\frac{19}{7} = \frac{7}{7} + \frac{7}{7} + \frac{5}{7} = 2\frac{5}{7}$

6 $\frac{15}{4} = \frac{4}{4} + \frac{4}{4} + \frac{4}{4} + \frac{3}{4} = 3\frac{3}{4}$

7 $\frac{19}{6} = \frac{6}{6} + \frac{6}{6} + \frac{6}{6} + \frac{1}{6} = 3\frac{1}{6}$

8 $\frac{11}{3} = \frac{3}{3} + \frac{3}{3} + \frac{3}{3} + \frac{2}{3} = 3\frac{2}{3}$

9 $\frac{7}{2} = \frac{2}{2} + \frac{2}{2} + \frac{2}{2} + \frac{1}{2} = 3\frac{1}{2}$

10 $\frac{12}{5} = \frac{5}{5} + \frac{5}{5} + \frac{2}{5} = 2\frac{2}{5}$

11 $2\frac{3}{4} = \frac{4}{4} + \frac{4}{4} + \frac{3}{4} = \frac{11}{4}$

12 $3\frac{2}{5} = \frac{5}{5} + \frac{5}{5} + \frac{5}{5} + \frac{2}{5} = \frac{17}{5}$

13 $1\frac{5}{7} = \frac{7}{7} + \frac{5}{7} = \frac{12}{7}$

14 $3\frac{1}{3} = \frac{3}{3} + \frac{3}{3} + \frac{3}{3} + \frac{1}{3} = \frac{10}{3}$

15 $4\frac{1}{2} = \frac{2}{2} + \frac{2}{2} + \frac{2}{2} + \frac{2}{2} + \frac{1}{2} = \frac{9}{2}$

16 $3\frac{1}{6} = \frac{6}{6} + \frac{6}{6} + \frac{6}{6} + \frac{1}{6} = \frac{19}{6}$

Adding and subtracting fractions (pp. 42–44)

1

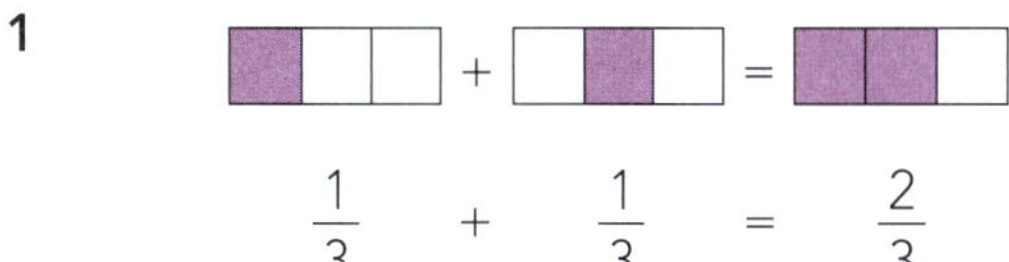

$\frac{1}{3} + \frac{1}{3} = \frac{2}{3}$

2

$\frac{2}{5} + \frac{2}{5} = \frac{4}{5}$

3

$\frac{1}{4} + \frac{2}{4} = \frac{3}{4}$

4

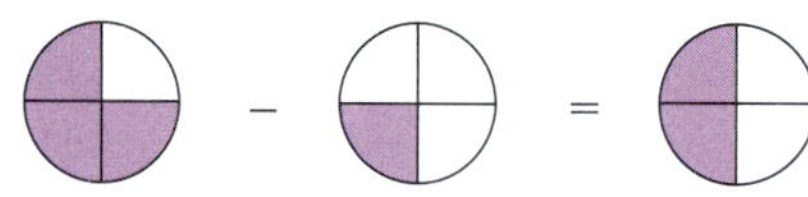

$\frac{3}{4} - \frac{1}{4} = \frac{2}{4}$

5

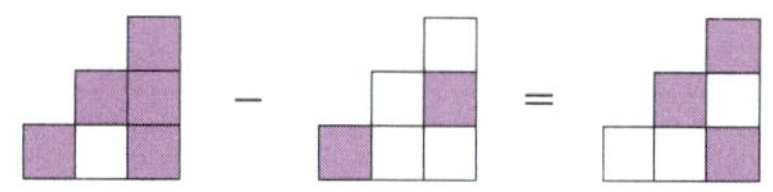

$\frac{5}{6} - \frac{2}{6} = \frac{3}{6}$

6

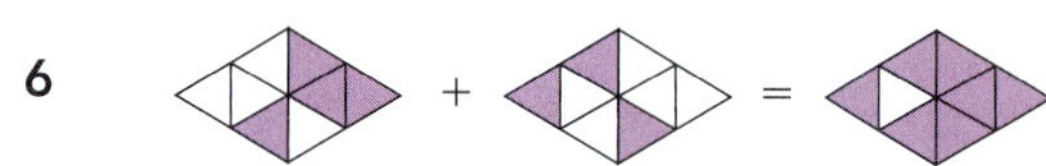

$\frac{4}{8} + \frac{3}{8} = \frac{7}{8}$

7 $\frac{4}{5}$ **8** $\frac{2}{8}$

9 $\frac{3}{6}$ **10** $\frac{1}{4}$

11

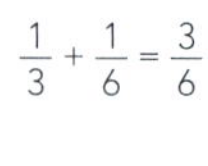

$\frac{1}{3} + \frac{1}{6} = \frac{3}{6}$

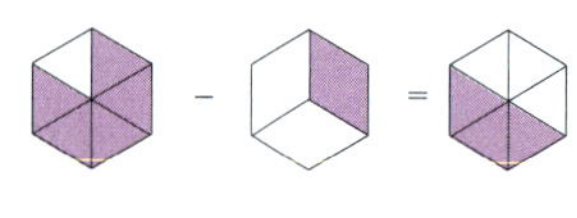

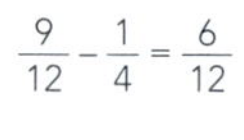

$\frac{9}{12} - \frac{1}{4} = \frac{6}{12}$

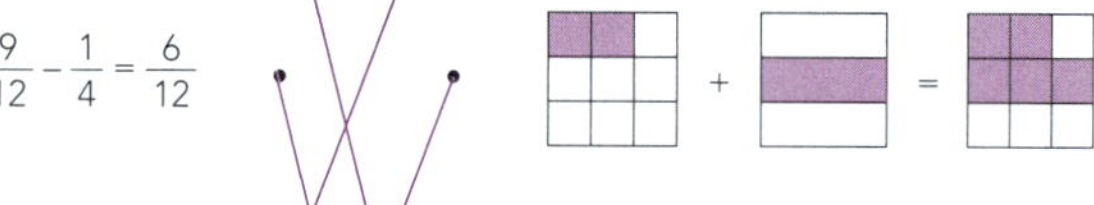

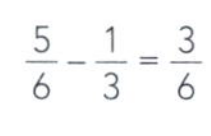

$\frac{5}{6} - \frac{1}{3} = \frac{3}{6}$

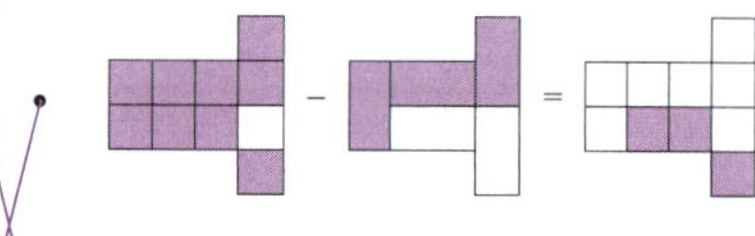

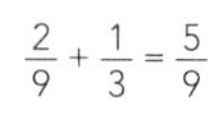

$\frac{2}{9} + \frac{1}{3} = \frac{5}{9}$

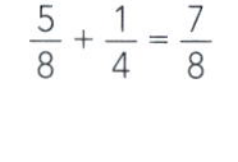

$\frac{5}{8} + \frac{1}{4} = \frac{7}{8}$

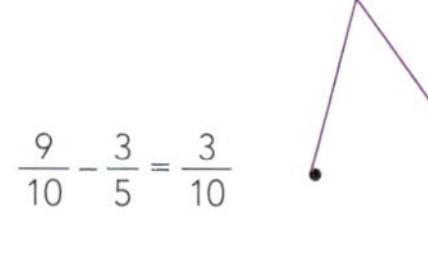

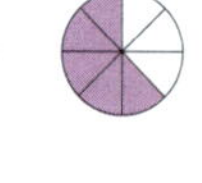

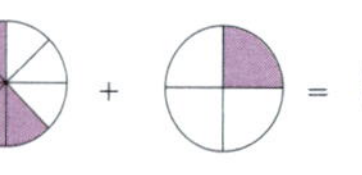

$\frac{9}{10} - \frac{3}{5} = \frac{3}{10}$

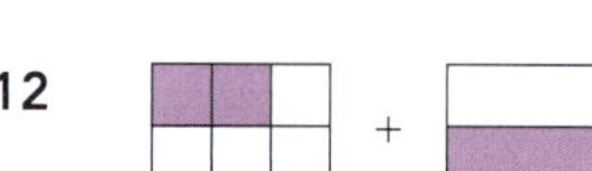

12

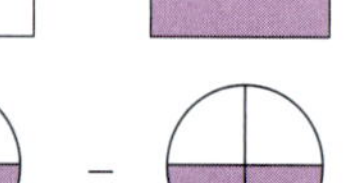

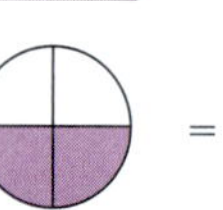

$\frac{2}{6} + \frac{1}{2} = \frac{5}{6}$

13

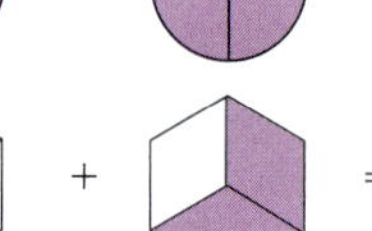

$\frac{3}{4} - \frac{1}{2} = \frac{1}{4}$

14

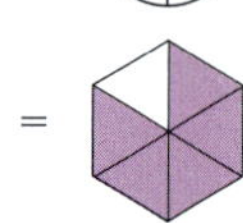

$\frac{1}{6} + \frac{2}{3} = \frac{5}{6}$

15

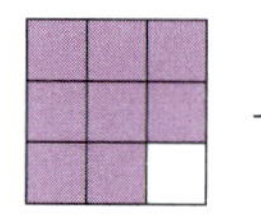

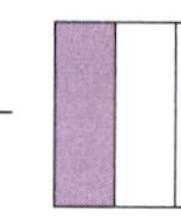

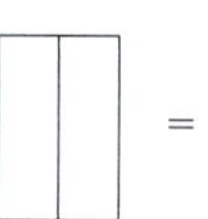

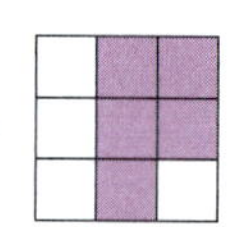

$\frac{8}{9} - \frac{1}{3} = \frac{5}{9}$

16

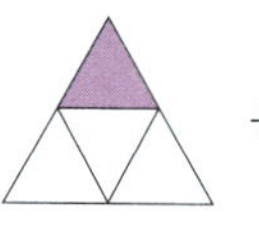

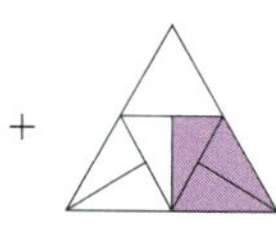

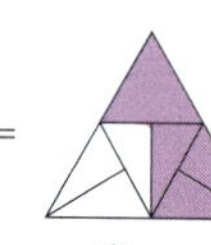

$\frac{1}{4} + \frac{3}{8} = \frac{5}{8}$

17

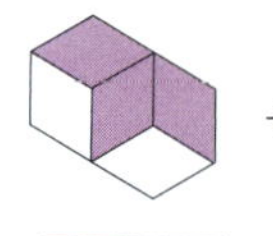

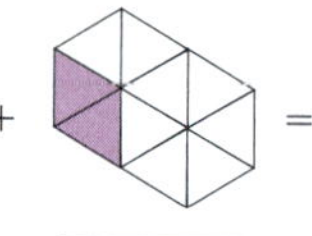

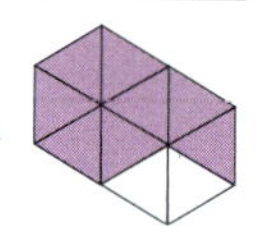

$\frac{3}{5} + \frac{2}{10} = \frac{8}{10}$ or $\frac{4}{5}$

18

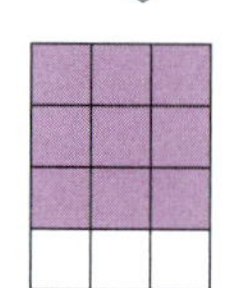

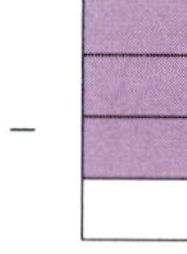

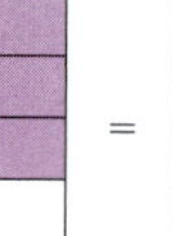

$\frac{9}{12} - \frac{3}{4} = 0$

Multiplying fractions (p. 45)

1 $\frac{1}{12}$ **2** $\frac{1}{5}$

3 $\frac{3}{20}$ **4** $\frac{3}{10}$

5 $\frac{6}{20} = \frac{3}{10}$ **6** $\frac{3}{48} = \frac{1}{16}$

7 $\frac{4}{35}$ **8** $\frac{6}{18} = \frac{1}{3}$

9 $\frac{3}{8}$ **10** $\frac{10}{12} = \frac{5}{6}$

Dividing fractions (pp. 46–47)

1 $\frac{3}{2}$ **2** $\frac{4}{1}$

3 $\frac{4}{5}$ **4** $\frac{6}{5}$

5 $\frac{8}{7}$ **6** $\frac{6}{8}$

7 $\frac{7}{4}$ **8** $\frac{1}{3}$

9 $\frac{3}{4}$ **10** $\frac{4}{7}$

11 $\frac{3}{4}$ **12** $\frac{5}{3} = 1\frac{2}{3}$

13 $\frac{18}{4} = 4\frac{1}{2}$ **14** $\frac{5}{12}$

15 $\frac{12}{5} = 2\frac{2}{5}$ **16** $\frac{6}{7}$

17 $\frac{12}{4} = 3$ **18** $\frac{10}{18} = \frac{5}{9}$

19 $\frac{20}{28} = \frac{5}{7}$ **20** $\frac{1}{25}$

21 $\frac{6}{1} = 6$ **22** $\frac{4}{15}$

 ISBN: 9780170447379

Fractions of a quantity (p. 48)

1 6 | 2 21
3 5 | 4 7
5 60 | 6 18
7 18 | 8 24
9 20 | 10 30

Mixing it up (p. 49)

1 $\frac{3}{5}$

2 $\frac{1}{4}$

3 $3\frac{1}{5}$

4 21

5 a $\frac{3}{20}$

b $\frac{4}{15}$

c $\frac{13}{10} = 1\frac{3}{10}$

d $\frac{17}{24}$

6 $\frac{19}{7}$

7 $\frac{4}{14}$ or $\frac{6}{21}$ or $\frac{8}{28}$

8 Shaded $\frac{3}{9} = \frac{1}{3}$ Not shaded $\frac{6}{9} = \frac{2}{3}$

9 $\frac{3}{10}$

10 $\frac{1}{4} = \frac{3}{12} = \frac{4}{16} = \frac{5}{20} = \frac{6}{24} = \frac{7}{28} = \frac{12}{48}$

Challenge 2 (p. 50)

1 Gillian ate $\frac{50}{75}$, Greg ate $\frac{48}{75}$.
Therefore Gillian ate more.

2 24

3 $\frac{2}{15}$

4 40

5

$\frac{4}{8} = \frac{1}{2}$	$\frac{1}{5} = \frac{2}{10}$	$\frac{3}{9} = \frac{1}{3}$
$\frac{2}{8} = \frac{1}{4}$	$\frac{5}{10} = \frac{1}{2}$	$\frac{3}{4} = \frac{9}{12}$
$\frac{2}{6} = \frac{1}{3}$	$\frac{1}{4} = \frac{3}{12}$	$\frac{2}{3} = \frac{6}{9}$

Decimals (pp. 51–60)

Place value (pp. 51–53)

		Number	Words
1	12 634	600	Six hundred
2	2 354 176	50 000	Fifty thousand
3	5 341	40	Forty
4	137 789 100	7 000 000	Seven million
5	810 240	800 000	Eight hundred thousand
6	561 266	1 000	One thousand
7	92 389	80	Eighty
8	217 431 891	200 000 000	Two hundred million
9	7 223	200	Two hundred
10	691 864 265	90 000 000	Ninety million

		Decimal	Fraction	Words
11	0.572	0.5	$\frac{5}{10}$	Five tenths
12	0.126	0.006	$\frac{6}{1\,000}$	Six thousandths
13	23.641	0.04	$\frac{4}{100}$	Four hundredths
14	198.153	0.003	$\frac{3}{1\,000}$	Three thousandths
15	6.108	0.008	$\frac{8}{1\,000}$	Eight thousandths
16	7.213	0.2	$\frac{2}{10}$	Two tenths
17	90.145	0.04	$\frac{4}{100}$	Four hundredths
18	0.029	0.009	$\frac{9}{1\,000}$	Nine thousandths

19 One thousand, two hundred and fifty-three
20 Fifty-two thousand, six hundred and seventy-four
21 Eight hundred and one
22 Twenty-five and seven tenths
23 Two hundred and forty-six thousand, one hundred and ninety-seven and eight tenths
24 Three hundred and one million, six hundred and forty-two thousand, one hundred and twenty-one
25 Twelve hundredths
26 Three hundred thousand, one hundred and ninety-two and nine tenths
27 One hundred thousand and one and forty-three hundredths
28 192
29 34.9
30 9 217
31 1 450 006
32 33 000
33 0.45
34 832.4
35 700 046
36 78 000 153.9

Decimals on number lines (pp. 54–55)

1

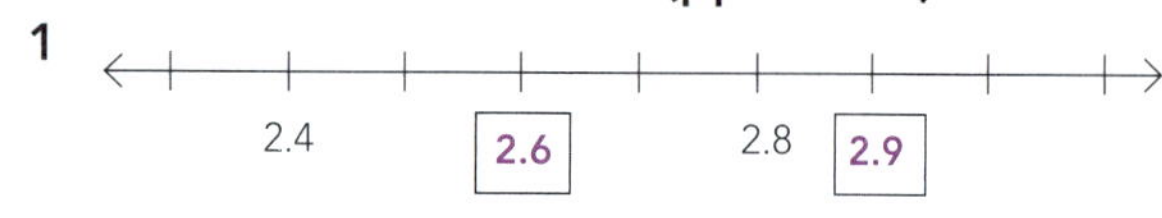

Size of gap = $\frac{2.8 - 2.4}{4} = \frac{0.4}{4} = 0.1$

2

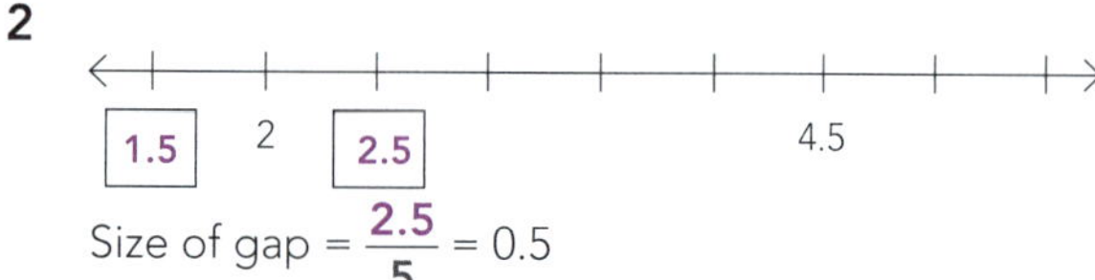

Size of gap = $\frac{2.5}{5} = 0.5$

3

5.4   6.0   6.4   6.8

Size of gap = $\frac{0.4}{2} = 0.2$

4

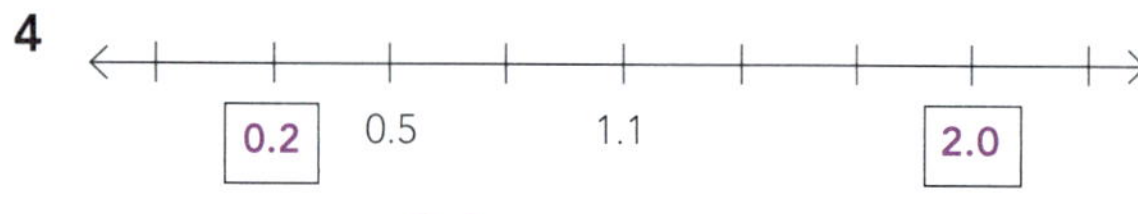

Size of gap = $\frac{0.6}{2} = 0.3$

5

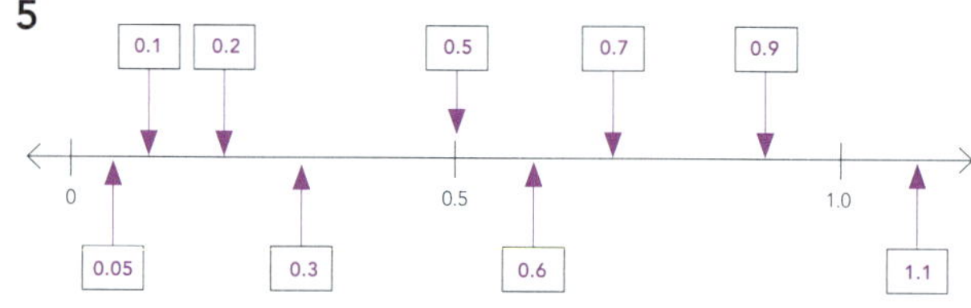

Challenge 3 (pp. 55–56)

1

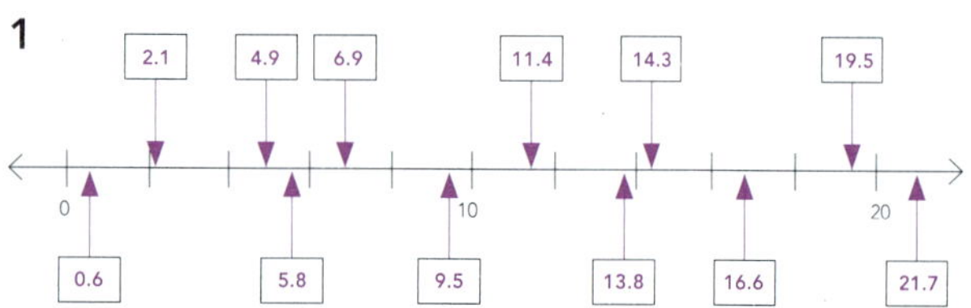

2

(1) 2	(2) 1	3	(3) 4	(4) 2	(5) 9	7	■	(6) 1
■	0	■	(7) 6	0	0	■	(8) 4	4
(9) 9	■	(10) 8	1	7	.	(11) 9	■	6
(12) 9	(13) 2	0	5	■	(14) 4	3	(15) 1	1
(16) 4	0	0	■	■	■	(17) 5	.	7
(18) 4	0	0	(19) 8	■	(20) 1	5	9	0
9	■	(21) 1	9	(22) 6	0	0	■	0
(23) 9	0	■	(24) 9	.	4	■	(25) 7	■
4	■	(26) 8	9	0	0	4	1	6

Comparing decimals (pp. 57–58)

1	**13.5**	13.4	**2**	1 457	**1 458**
3	**9.52**	9.51	**4**	56.46	**56.47**
5	423.8	**423.9**	**6**	**8.41**	8.40
7	101.0	**110.0**	**8**	6.01	**6.10**
9	0.94	**0.95**	**10**	0.67	**0.76**
11	equal		**12**	8.47	**8.74**
13	8.2		**14**	44.6	
15	40.5		**16**	60.84	
17	6 463		**18**	434.1	
19	0.38		**20**	86.2	
21	1 257	7 521	**22**	20 689	98 620
23	124 689	986 421	**24**	103	310
25	1 012 349	9 432 110	**26**	5.16, 5.61, 6.15, 6.51	
27	0.00, 0.01, 0.10, 0.11		**28**	4.11, 4.14, 4.41, 4.44	
29	0.88, 0.89, 0.98, 0.99		**30**	0.02, 0.20, 2.00, 2.02	

Using decimals to compare fractions (pp. 59–60)

1	0.6 0.7	$\frac{14}{20}$ is larger than $\frac{3}{5}$
2	0.44 0.45	$\frac{9}{20}$ is larger than $\frac{11}{25}$
3	0.75 0.74	$\frac{3}{4}$ is larger than $\frac{37}{50}$
4	0.52 0.54	$\frac{27}{50}$ is larger than $\frac{13}{25}$
5	0.11 0.1	$\frac{11}{100}$ is larger than $\frac{8}{80}$
6	0.328125 0.3125	$\frac{21}{64}$ is larger than $\frac{5}{16}$
7	0.88 0.875	$\frac{22}{25}$ is larger than $\frac{7}{8}$
8	0.375 0.38	$\frac{19}{50}$ is larger than $\frac{3}{8}$
9	0.4375 0.438	$\frac{219}{500}$ is larger than $\frac{7}{16}$
10	0.34375 0.34376	$\frac{4297}{12500}$ is larger than $\frac{22}{64}$
11	0.25 0.255	$\frac{51}{200}$ is larger than $\frac{1}{4}$
12	1.15 1.2	$\frac{6}{5}$ is larger than $\frac{23}{20}$
13	1.52 1.51	$\frac{38}{25}$ is larger than $\frac{151}{100}$
14	2.642 2.64	$\frac{1321}{500}$ is larger than $\frac{66}{25}$

ISBN: 9780170447379

15

Start

$\frac{1}{10}$	$\frac{2}{25}$	$\frac{13}{100}$	$\frac{4}{10}$	$\frac{6}{12}$	$\frac{17}{20}$	$\frac{32}{97}$
$\frac{1}{9}$	**$\frac{3}{25}$**	**$\frac{7}{50}$**	$\frac{1}{50}$	$\frac{12}{25}$	$\frac{13}{20}$	$\frac{4}{5}$
$\frac{3}{50}$	$\frac{4}{40}$	**$\frac{3}{20}$**	$\frac{26}{200}$	**$\frac{29}{50}$**	**$\frac{3}{4}$**	**$\frac{41}{50}$**
$\frac{33}{200}$	**$\frac{41}{250}$**	**$\frac{81}{500}$**	$\frac{4}{25}$	**$\frac{11}{20}$**	$\frac{27}{50}$	**$\frac{17}{20}$**
$\frac{1}{5}$	$\frac{4}{25}$	$\frac{161}{1000}$	**$\frac{12}{25}$**	**$\frac{9}{18}$**	$\frac{12}{25}$	**$\frac{18}{20}$**
$\frac{11}{50}$	**$\frac{7}{20}$**	**$\frac{2}{5}$**	**$\frac{23}{50}$**	$\frac{11}{25}$	$\frac{30}{50}$	**$\frac{99}{100}$**

Finish

Percentages (pp. 61–72)

1 Percentage purple 53%
Percentage white 47%

2 Percentage purple 7%
Percentage white 93%

3 Percentage purple 20%
Percentage white 80%

4 Percentage purple 13%
Percentage white 87%

5 Percentage dark purple 15%
Percentage light purple 10%
Percentage white 75%

6 Percentage dark purple 14%
Percentage light purple 26%
Percentage white 60%

7 Percentage purple $\frac{21}{50} \times 100 = 42\%$

Percentage white $\frac{29}{50} \times 100 = 58\%$

8 Percentage purple $\frac{18}{50} \times 100 = 36\%$

Percentage white $\frac{32}{50} \times 100 = 64\%$

9 Percentage purple $\frac{12}{30} \times 100 = 40\%$

Percentage white $\frac{18}{30} \times 100 = 60\%$

10 Percentage purple $\frac{18}{30} \times 100 = 60\%$

Percentage white $\frac{12}{30} \times 100 = 40\%$

11 Percentage purple $\frac{12}{15} \times 100 = 80\%$

Percentage white $\frac{3}{15} \times 100 = 20\%$

12 Percentage purple $\frac{8}{16} \times 100 = 50\%$

Percentage white $\frac{8}{16} \times 100 = 50\%$

13

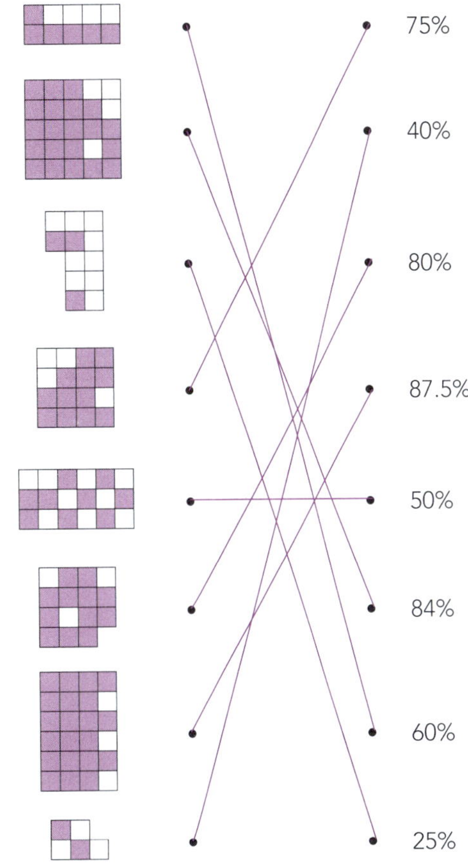

Converting between fractions and percentages (pp. 64–65)

1 30% **2** 20%
3 30% **4** 75%
5 85% **6** 92%
7 6% **8** 95%
9 40% **10** 67%
11 87.5% **12** 13.6%
13 180% **14** 125%

15 $\frac{6}{25}$ **16** $\frac{3}{4}$
17 $\frac{13}{100}$ **18** $\frac{4}{5}$
19 $\frac{11}{20}$ **20** $\frac{1}{10}$
21 $\frac{31}{50}$ **22** $\frac{49}{50}$
23 $\frac{7}{100}$ **24** $\frac{1}{25}$
25 $\frac{1}{100}$ **26** $\frac{53}{20}$
27 $\frac{1}{1}$ **28** $\frac{6}{5}$

What's my number? (p. 65)

1 0.45 **2** 20%

ISBN: 9780170447379

Converting between decimals and percentages (pp. 66–67)

1	25%	**2**	40%
3	32%	**4**	69%
5	13%	**6**	99%
7	87%	**8**	11%
9	51%	**10**	75%
11	26%	**12**	9%
13	36.5%	**14**	3%
15	100%	**16**	120%
17	600%	**18**	134%
19	0.63	**20**	0.52
21	0.99	**22**	0.14
23	0.80	**24**	0.22
25	0.38	**26**	0.99
27	0.1	**28**	0.78
29	0.485	**30**	0.327
31	1.30 or 1.3	**32**	2.00 or 2
33	0.5		

Converting between fractions, decimals and percentages (p. 68)

	Fraction	Decimal	Percentage
1	$\frac{1}{2}$	0.5	50%
2	$\frac{3}{5}$	0.6	60%
3	$\frac{1}{5}$	0.2	20%
4	$\frac{1}{4}$	0.25	25%
5	$\frac{2}{5}$	0.4	40%
6	$\frac{4}{5}$	0.8	80%
7	$\frac{7}{20}$	0.35	35%
8	$\frac{3}{4}$	0.75	75%
9	$\frac{3}{10}$	0.3	30%
10	$\frac{7}{7}$	1.0	100%
11	$\frac{3}{8}$	0.375	37.5%
12	$\frac{1}{8}$	0.125	12.5%
13	$\frac{11}{20}$	0.55	55%
14	$\frac{7}{8}$	0.875	87.5%
15	$\frac{11}{10}$	1.10	110%

Challenge 4 (p. 69)

1

40%	$\frac{9}{20}$	0.35	~~30%~~	$\frac{4}{8}$	0.48	$\frac{23}{50}$	42%
0.4	0.45	0.35	0.30	0.5	0.48	0.46	0.42

Smallest → Largest

30%	0.35	40%	42%	$\frac{9}{20}$	$\frac{23}{50}$	0.48	$\frac{4}{8}$

2

81%	$\frac{41}{50}$	0.86	79%	$\frac{4}{5}$	0.84	$\frac{17}{20}$	89%
0.81	0.82	0.86	0.79	0.8	0.84	0.85	0.89

Smallest → Largest

79%	$\frac{4}{5}$	81%	$\frac{41}{50}$	0.84	$\frac{17}{20}$	0.86	89%

3

$\frac{3}{25}$	0.10	$\frac{7}{50}$	11%	0.13	$\frac{6}{40}$	0.16	10.5%
0.12	0.10	0.14	0.11	0.13	0.15	0.16	0.105

Smallest → Largest

0.10	10.5%	11%	$\frac{3}{25}$	0.13	$\frac{7}{50}$	$\frac{6}{40}$	0.16

4

65%	$\frac{5}{8}$	0.63	$\frac{16}{25}$	65.5%	0.654	$\frac{129}{200}$	0.66
0.65	0.625	0.63	0.64	0.655	0.654	0.645	0.66

Smallest → Largest

$\frac{5}{8}$	0.63	$\frac{16}{25}$	$\frac{129}{200}$	65%	0.654	65.5%	0.66

Calculating percentages (p. 70)

1	85%	**2**	72%
3	20%	**4**	14%
5	70%	**6**	10%
7	25%	**8**	64%
9	63.5%	**10**	22.22%
11	8%	**12**	25.24%

Finding percentages of amounts (pp. 71–72)

1	4	**2**	9
3	75	**4**	520
5	299	**6**	102
7	33	**8**	200 000
9	141	**10**	216
11	14.3	**12**	1 968
13	103.4	**14**	67.2
15	90	**16**	14 000
17	57	**18**	36
19	26		
20			

Start

12% of 50 = 6	**55% of 60 = 33**	20% of 60 = 10	9% of 10 = 10	25% of 92 = 22	32% of 50 = 15	16% of 800 = 18.2
60% of 84 = 50	**45% of 56 = 25.2**	**10% of 70 = 7**	59% of 30 = 27	80% of 65 = 51	45% of 22 = 9	70% of 64 = 48
25% of 83 = 20.2	11% of 88 = 10	**13% of 30 = 3.9**	33% of 70 = 21	40% of 30 = 10	7% of 40 = 2	28% of 60 = 18
15% of 20 = 3	**26% of 85 = 22.1**	**70% of 40 = 28**	26% of 95 = 27.4	**50% of 67 = 33.5**	**2% of 75 = 1.5**	**16% of 125 = 20**
40% of 67 = 26.8	92% of 35 = 33	35% of 52 = 12.8	6% of 35 = 2.2	**27% of 40 = 10.8**	76% of 40 = 34	**1% of 150 = 1.5**
85% of 20 = 17	**8% of 65 = 5.2**	**30% of 80 = 24**	46% of 45 = 19	**98% of 40 = 39.2**	30% of 30 = 10	**70% of 85 = 59.5**
26% of 85 = 22.2	43% of 76 = 30	**63% of 50 = 31.5**	**18% of 75 = 13.5**	**42% of 50 = 21**	27% of 50 = 15	**90% of 90 = 81**

Finish

ISBN: 9780170447379

Mixing it up (p. 73)

1 a 30, thirty b 0.06, six hundredths

2 a 47.5 b 0.8

3 a $\frac{4}{5}$ or $\frac{41}{50}$ b $\frac{7}{8}$ or 85%

c 0.45 or $\frac{11}{25}$ d 0.3 or $\frac{1}{3}$

4 2.13, 2.31, 3.12, 3.21

5 a 45%

b 55%

6 Sixty-two thousand, eight hundred and fifty-three

7 13

8 65%

9 8412

10

10%	$\frac{3}{25}$	0.13	15%	$\frac{3}{50}$	0.21	$\frac{1}{5}$	22%
0.1	0.12	0.13	0.15	0.06	0.21	0.2	0.22

Smallest → Largest

$\frac{3}{50}$	10%	$\frac{3}{25}$	0.13	15%	$\frac{1}{5}$	0.21	22%

Word questions (p. 74)

1 75%

2 $\frac{3}{18}$ or $\frac{1}{6}$

3 25% of 40 lollies (10) because it is more than $\frac{3}{8}$ of 24 (9).

4 $4.80

5 16

6 $\frac{16}{15}$ or $1\frac{1}{15}$

7 9

8 35%

9 Jeremy 70% and Lucy 64%, therefore Jeremy did better.

10 6 days

Rounding (pp. 75–79)

Rounding to whole numbers (pp. 75–77)

1

	Rounded to the nearest:	Highlight the last required digit	Answer
147	ten	147	150
46 912	thousand	46 912	47 000
9 251	hundred	9 251	9 300
2 456 987	thousand	2 456 987	2 457 000
987 215	ten	987 125	987 130
53 143	hundred	53 143	53 100

2

	Nearest ten	Nearest hundred	Nearest thousand
5 184	5 180	5 200	5 000
16 735	16 740	16 700	17 000
221 264	221 260	221 300	221 000
3 864	3 860	3 900	4 000
28 612	28 610	28 600	29 000
1 352 765	1 352 770	1 352 800	1 353 000
685 555	685 560	685 600	686 000

3 80

4 930

5 12 010

6 70

7 100

8 34 300

9 459 300

10 8 032 900

11 2 000

12 18 000

13 1 000

14 126 000

15 760 000

16 75 060 000

17 8 170 000

18 10 000

19 1 000 000

20 3 000 000

21 78 000 000

22 100 000 000

23

Original number	Rounded to the nearest:	Rounded number
268	tens	270
6 384	thousands	6 000
8 155	tens	8 160
342 179	hundreds	342 200
71 656	thousands	72 000
12 648 544	ten thousands	12 650 000
6 895	hundreds	6 900
2 356 999	millions	2 000 000

Rounding decimals (pp. 78–79)

1 2 dp; 1 dp; 0 dp; 3 dp; 1 dp; 2 dp; 3 dp

2

	Rounded to the nearest:	Highlight the last required digit	Answer
38.541	1 dp	38.541	38.5
1.2678	3 dp	1.2678	1.268
92.03541	4 dp	92.03541	92.0354
9.562	2 dp	9.562	9.56
126.426	1 dp	126.426	126.4
86.31	0 dp	86.31	86
5.3288	3 dp	5.3288	5.329
0.486	2 dp	0.486	0.49

ISBN: 9780170447379

3

	0 dp	1 dp	2 dp
5.67301	6	5.7	5.67
12.5555	13	12.6	12.56
6.6439	7	6.6	6.64
0.9276	1	0.9	0.93
1.0753	1	1.1	1.08
352.106	352	352.1	352.11
0.01489	0	0.0	0.01

4

	Rounded to the nearest:	Answer	Correct or round appropriately
0.0635	1 dp	0.06	Incorrect 0.1
50.4268	3 dp	50.427	Correct
845.1249	2 dp	845.13	Incorrect 845.12
0.003568	3 dp	0.0004	Incorrect 0.004

Estimations/approximations (p. 80)

1 1 + 6 = 7

2 11 + 2 = 13

3 15 – 8 = 7

4 9 – 3 = 6

5 28 + 1 + 4 = 33

6 10 + 2 + 17 = 29

7 13 + 5 – 3 = 15

8 15 – 5 + 1 = 11

9 2 x 8 =16

10 15 x 3 =45

11 $\frac{20}{5} = 4$

12 16 ÷ 2 =8

13 9 x 2 ÷ 3 = 6

14 8 ÷ 2 x 3 = 12

Challenge 5 (p. 81)

1

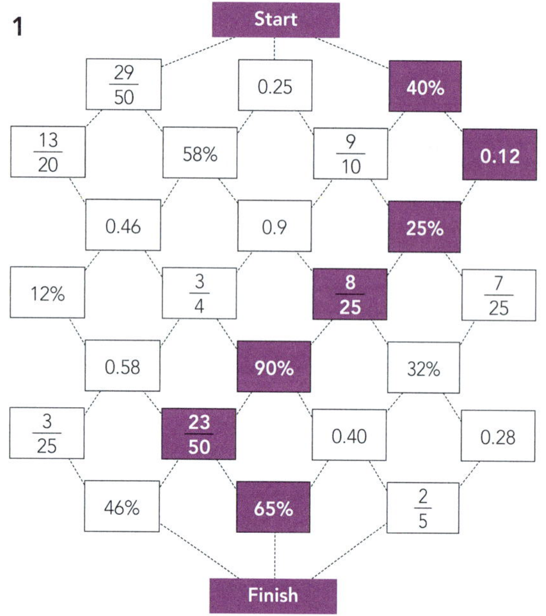

2 20% of 40 is 8

0.3 of 50 is 15

$\frac{4}{5}$ of 25 is 20

0.4 of 70 is 28

60% of 45 is 27

$\frac{2}{7}$ of 56 is 16

Revision 1 (pp. 82–84)

1 a 19 b 1.75

2 Yes; it has no factors other than 1 and itself.

3 100

4 1, 3, 5, 9, 15, 45

5 

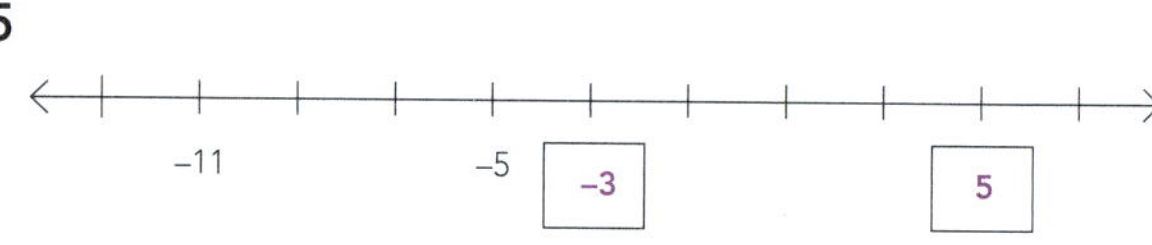

6 a 16 b 11

c 243 d 5

7 a 2 b 5

c 13 d 7

8 $\frac{4}{10}, \frac{6}{15}, \frac{8}{20}, \frac{10}{25}$

If yours isn't listed, check with your teacher.

9 a $\frac{5}{8}$ b $\frac{5}{6}$

c $\frac{2}{20} = \frac{1}{10}$ d $\frac{18}{8}$ or $2\frac{2}{8}$ or $2\frac{1}{4}$

10 a 12 b 40

11 a Twelve thousand, nine hundred and twenty-one

b Two and sixty-four hundredths

12 a 632 b 81 506

13 a $\frac{17}{25}$ b $\frac{5}{6}$

c 45% d 0.545

14

	Fraction	Decimal	Percentage
a	$\frac{3}{5}$	0.6	60%
b	$\frac{7}{20}$	0.35	35%
c	$\frac{4}{5}$ or $\frac{8}{10}$	0.8	80%
d	$\frac{9}{8}$	1.125	112.5

 ISBN: 9780170447379

15 a 12.72 b 506.6

16

	0 dp	1 dp	2 dp
6.5539	7	6.6	6.55
439.1068	439	439.1	439.11

17 shaded = $\frac{7}{10}$ shaded = 70%

not shaded = $\frac{3}{10}$ not shaded = 30%

18

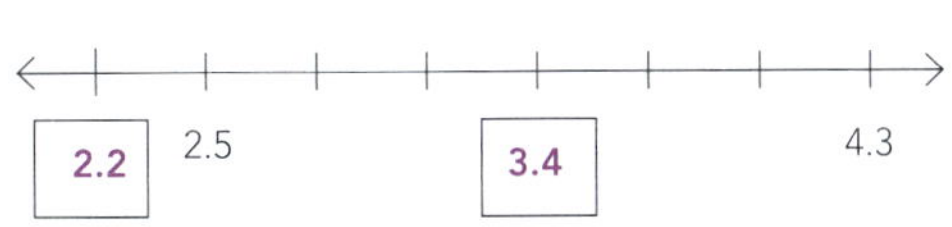

19

	Nearest ten	Nearest hundred	Nearest thousand
1 936	1 940	1 900	2 000
27 085	27 090	27 100	27 000
745 689	745 690	745 700	746 000

20 4.45, 4.54, 5.45, 5.54

21

80%	$\frac{5}{6}$	0.79	$\frac{39}{50}$	77%	0.81	$\frac{21}{25}$	75%
0.8	0.8333	0.79	0.78	0.77	0.81	0.84	0.75

Smallest Largest

75%	77%	$\frac{39}{50}$	0.79	80%	0.81	$\frac{5}{6}$	$\frac{21}{25}$

22 $\frac{5}{12}$

23 32%

Revision 2 (pp. 85–87)

1 a 21 b 2

2 Yes; it has no factors other than 1 and itself.

3 12

4 6, 12, 18, 24, 30

5

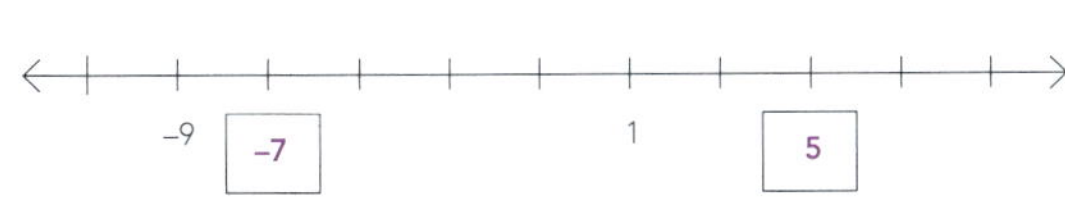

6 a 27 b 8
c 32 d 6

7 a 3 b 3
c 11 d 1

8 $\frac{4}{6}, \frac{6}{9}, \frac{8}{12}, \frac{10}{15}$

If yours isn't listed, check with your teacher.

9 a $\frac{3}{5}$ b $\frac{5}{7}$

c $\frac{2}{12} = \frac{1}{6}$ d $\frac{25}{12}$ or $2\frac{1}{12}$

10 a 24.8 b 44

11 a Nine thousand, one hundred and fifty-four

b Twenty-three hundredths

12 a 483 b 53 402

13 a $\frac{2}{3}$ b 0.62

c 29% d 0.2314

14

	Fraction	Decimal	Percentage
a	$\frac{1}{5}$	0.2	20%
b	$\frac{9}{10}$	0.9	90%
c	$\frac{1}{4}$	0.25	25%
d	$\frac{6}{5}$	1.2	120%

15 a 8.3 b 199.1

16

	0 dp	1 dp	2 dp
1.3468	1	1.3	1.35
964.0561	964	964.1	964.06

17 shaded = $\frac{11}{20}$ shaded = 55%

not shaded = $\frac{9}{20}$ not shaded = 45%

18

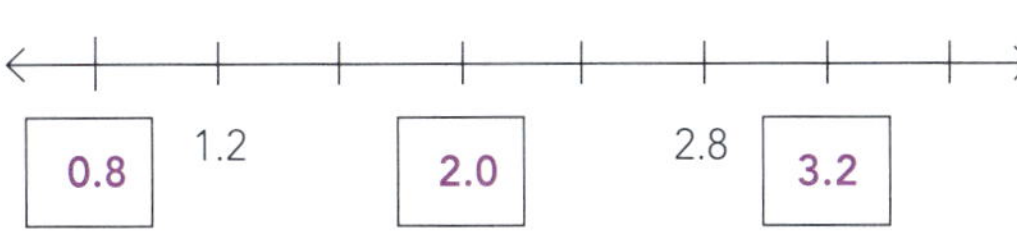

19

	Nearest ten	Nearest hundred	Nearest thousand
3 647	3 650	3 600	4 000
12 876	12 880	12 900	13 000
684 023	684 020	684 000	684 000

20 8.09, 8.90, 9.08, 9.80

21

20%	$\frac{1}{4}$	0.30	$\frac{13}{50}$	19%	0.21	$\frac{6}{25}$	27%
0.2	0.25	0.30	0.26	0.19	0.21	0.24	0.27

Smallest — Largest

19%	20%	0.21	$\frac{6}{25}$	$\frac{1}{4}$	$\frac{13}{50}$	27%	0.30

22 $\frac{1}{5}$

23 37.5%

 ISBN: 9780170447379